The Prentice Hall Mini-Series in Music E(
Edited by Richard J. Colwell

MW01061330

The Prentice Hall Mini-Series in Music Education offers a flexible approach to preparing teachers for success in the music classroom. The series provides succinctly written texts covering the information needed, first, to qualify for teacher certification in music education, and second, to adapt to the increasingly broad and diverse demands placed on the teacher in today's schools. A third focus is to enable the classroom teacher to appropriately integrate music with other instruction to reach the objectives of music teaching and learning. The range of topics in the series emphasizes the goals of a valid music program, beginning with pre-kindergarten, a program that is varied and flexible without sacrificing competence in musical skills, understanding, and knowledge.

Already Published

An Orientation to Music Education	Richard J. Colwell and Lizabeth Bradford Wing
Musical Lives of Young Children	John W. Flohr
Sociology for Music Teachers: Perspectives for Practice	Hildegard C. Froehlich
Technology for Music Educators	Fred Rees

Forthcoming

Improvisation	Sandra Stauffer
Perspectives on Music Cognition	Lyle Davidson
Music Education in the Middle School	Tim Gerber

Sociology for Music Teachers

Perspectives for Practice

Hildegard C. Froehlich

Upper Saddle River, New Jersey 07458

Library of Congress Cataloging-in-Publication Data

Froehlich, Hildegard C.

Sociology for music teachers : perspectives for practice / Hildegard C. Froehlich.
  p. cm.
Includes bibliographical references and index.
  ISBN 0-13-177696-7
1. Music—Instruction and study—Social aspects.   2. Music—Social aspects.
3. Educational sociology.   I. Title.
MT1.F79 2007   2006046171
306.4'842—dc22

Editor-in-Chief: Sarah Touborg
Executive Editor: Richard Carlin
Editorial Assistant: Jeanmarie Ensor
Marketing Manager: Andrea Messineo
Director of Production & Manufacturing: Barbara Kittle
Managing Editor: Lisa Iarkowski
Production Editor: Jean Lapidus
Manufacturing Buyer: Benjamin D. Smith
Copy Editor: Anne Lesser
Indexer: Murray Fisher
Cover Design: Bruce Kenselaar
Cover Printer: Courier/Stoughton
Compositor: Techbooks
Printer/Binder: Courier/Stoughton

Credits and acknowledgments borrowed from other sources and reproduced, with permission, in this textbook appear on appropriate page within text.

Pearson Education LTD.   Pearson Education Australia PTY, Limited
Pearson Education Singapore, Pte. Ltd   Pearson Education North Asia Ltd
Pearson Education Canada, Ltd   Pearson Educación de Mexico, S.A. de C.V.
Pearson Education—Japan   Pearson Education Malaysia, Pte. Ltd

10 9 8 7 6 5 4 3 2 1
ISBN: 0-13-177696-7

Contents

Acknowledgments and Dedication

While acknowledgements open a book, they actually are the author's last words in a long process of thinking, writing, re-writing, editing, and writing again. Such a process requires the help of committed colleagues and friends. I am fortunate that I was able to call on many.

First and foremost, my special thanks go to Marie McCarthy not only for having been responsible for involving me in this project more than five years ago but also for her support and constructive comments in many of the earlier drafts. The later stages of the manuscripts were critically accompanied by Richard Colwell's detailed editorial comments and probing questions. I also thank Lee Bartel, Anthony Palmer, Thomas Regelski, Roger Rideout, and Brian Roberts for reading versions of the manuscript and for making many constructive suggestions for its improvement. I heeded their advice as much as this book's space limitations allowed but also acknowledge that I chose to leave certain concerns unattended.

Turning a manuscript into book form is a formidable task, no matter what the size of the book. I therefore owe a word of gratitude to the staff of Pearson Prentice Hall, namely Jean Lapidus, who proved invaluable as overseer of a process that can be difficult but, thanks to her and her colleagues, turned out to be a calming and reassuring experience.

Finally, my special thanks go to John McDonnell Tierney, Ph.D., author of *Making Sense in the Field of Time and Space. Reflections on the Education of Young Human Beings* (2003), a book that contains many wise insights about the art of teaching. His permission to use selected aphorisms at the beginning of each of my chapters is much appreciated.

The book is dedicated to my undergraduate and graduate students at the University of North Texas. Over the 25 years during which I taught a sociology of music course, they had repeatedly asked me when I might put on paper some of the issues they considered especially relevant to their work as music educators. I hope I fulfilled their expectations.

Hildegard C. Froehlich

Introduction

Why Look at Music Teaching
from a Sociological Perspective?

The question heading this introductory chapter often is asked by people who wonder why musicians need knowledge of society at large to be fine music teachers, a question to which this book provides a possible answer. Most immediately, of course, sociologists do not generally engage in questions of *how* to teach music. But sociological thinking can clarify our own beliefs about *why* and *what* we teach. We learn to understand our own actions as the result of larger cultural, political, and economic constellations that shape our country's societal values and sociocultural traditions.

The field of music education is by its very nature interdisciplinary because school music teaching is imbedded in two major societal traditions: (1) the tradition of music making, listening, and responding; and (2) the tradition of education as a societal mandate. The first tradition holds firmly to music artistry and musicological scholarship, the latter including music sociology. The second tradition, that of education as a field of study, relies mostly on pedagogical principles rooted equally in psychology and sociology. I base this book on the premise that both traditions shape a music teacher's work.

General sociologists have not only addressed the place of music in society but have also, along with music sociologists, examined the different roles musicians assume as professionals in society. Furthermore, sociologists have contributed to the ongoing debates about music as a social force in the world of entertainment on the one hand and as a complex system of musical aesthetics on the other, issues with which music teachers are quite familiar. They know that in both of these worlds specific cultural values are developed, affirmed, and upheld.

1

As bridge builders between the worlds of professional music making and formal school education, music teachers' instructional choices not only reflect what curriculum committees, textbooks, and subject matter experts advocate but also what political, cultural, and economical influences mandate. In music teaching, social, educational, and musical values fall together.

Earlier histories of sociology focused on explanations of how society at large impacted social groups and individuals; today's sociologists acknowledge the reciprocal relationship between each individual in society and the traditions that shape any one social group and its members in society. In fact, Agger (2004) reminds us that sociology begins and ends "with the self, the person who lives in Arlington, Texas, or Arlington, Virginia; Eugene, Oregon; Topeka, Kansas; Toronto, Canada" (p. 4). It starts with how each of us sees society and our place in it. Inevitably, this knowledge is specific to how each of us has been shaped by family, peer, and other influences, both genetic and environmental. Such knowledge is context bound and develops long before we enter school, impacting forever the rest of our lives socially, culturally, and musically.

To some extent, music students in college and experienced music teachers alike are already familiar with these societal givens. However, thanks to work done over the past fifty years by sociologists, ethnomusicologists, cultural theorists, educational philosophers, and social psychologists, our awareness has grown about the sociocultural and sociopolitical contexts that frame our work as music teachers. We know that certain types of music learning and teaching processes can be threatening to one group of people while it affirms another group's lifestyle and value system. School music teachers face such differences in value systems firsthand.

Take, for example, a middle-school student during rehearsal who asks, "Why can't we ever sing *good* songs in class?" Does this question suggest boredom, a musically inquisitive mind, or a student who feels alienated from the learning process and therefore may become a potential troublemaker? Conversely, do well-behaved students truly share our enthusiasm for the music we perform or have they learned, at times grudgingly, to go along with what teachers ask from them?

The best way to gain insight into these questions is by knowing not only the social and cultural backgrounds of our students but also our own. We need to ask ourselves how and why our own musical and educational values evolved the way they did and how both shape our actions as musicians and pedagogues. Such knowledge can then lead to a greater ability to understand the reasons behind value systems other than our own, the first step in better communicative skills.

The Purpose of This Book

The book is aimed at aspiring music teacher candidates and experienced music teachers returning for advanced degrees in music education. It seeks to inform them about the contributions general sociologists as well sociologists of education have made to our understanding of how society shapes the role of the teacher, the student, and the school curriculum of which music is but a small part.

To make this point, the first chapter focuses on how music teachers reportedly have become who they are, both as musicians and pedagogues. Based on the work by music educators as well as sociologists in education, the chapter leads to a more general description of teaching as work in the institutional setting of school (Chapter 2). Chapter 3 further details music teaching and learning as social phenomena and provides three major sociological perspectives by which to examine the place of music learning and teaching in society. The application of these perspectives to music education is a recurring theme throughout the book and is the explicit reason for Chapter 4, an overview of selected texts in the sociology of music.

The overview, along with Chapter 5, forms the background information needed to engage in debates about the purpose of music in the curriculum. Although few music sociologists have directly addressed music education as one of their concerns, they have extensively argued about the *art* of music for its own sake vis-à-vis music as a form of socially situated behavior. It is a discussion about relative versus absolute musical values, a topic that shapes today's philosophical debates in music education as much as it did yesterday's.

Because music teachers do not only live in the world of music but also in the world of education, philosophical debates cannot remain in the realm of music alone. They must equally consider the world of education. It is for this reason that Chapter 6 provides an introduction to the sociology of education, a field vast in itself because of the many extant viewpoints on the purpose and function of formal education in society. The chapter makes the point that the perspective one chooses to answer such questions also impacts how one teaches a particular subject matter. Chapter 7 shows the application of such thinking to music-teaching realities and practices.

I do not and cannot prescribe recipes that work for everybody because each teacher faces circumstances that are contextually bound and therefore unique. Rather, the practicality of this book may come from a teacher's deepening sense of how prevailing cultural values interconnect with schools and their curricula and how such connections impact one's work. Educational mandates and musical traditions, along with today's students' musical preferences and listening habits, form the realities within which music teachers make their pedagogical choices. This book describes the realities as sociologists have examined them.

College classes vary in student composition and collective interest. This fact makes it likely that not all chapters will be equally useful to all students and an instructor's course objectives. I therefore recommend selective use of the chapters in an order that fits the needs of a particular course.

Throughout the book I seek to place broader conceptual issues into the immediacy of specific tasks. Identified as small group discussions, writing tasks, observation and interview projects, and questions for class discussion, the tasks are intended to facilitate opportunities to question accepted teaching modalities where necessary and, where appropriate, to affirm "the tried and proven."

Some of the suggested tasks are more time consuming than others. The interview projects in particular might constitute a semester-long assignment and perhaps become the basis for an actual research project. Therefore, which tasks to choose should be decided carefully and jointly between each student and the course instructor. Needless to say, all tasks are suggestions only. Others can be substituted. But I consider it essential that the students engage in hands-on tasks while reading the book.

Finally, terms and names included in the index are boldfaced the first time they appear in the text. The symbol (**D**) after a term points to an operational definition in Selected Definitions at the end of the book.

The Book's Historical Frame

In 1938, musicologist Eli Siegmeister began his essay *Music and Society* with an expression of astonishment, "that at this late date the place of music in society and the influence of social forces on its development have been so little studied" (Siegmeister, 1938/1974), p. 9). Similar sentiments were voiced most notably in the late 1950s and mid-1960s by sociologists John Mueller (1895–1965) and Max Kaplan (1911–1999).

Mueller (1958) saw a need for sociological analyses in examining many aspects relevant to the reality of music teaching. Among them were (1) aesthetic systems of thought expressed by musicians and laypeople, (2) the nature of music as perceived by different groups of people, (3) the notion that the arts are "naturally" interrelated, (4) the social nature of musical taste, and (5) the functions of music and education. The issue of musical taste led Mueller to conduct some empirical studies on the nature of musical taste, as much a psychological as a sociological question. Kaplan first articulated the need for a sociology of music and music education in his dissertation (1951, 1952) and later in *Foundations and Frontiers of Music Education* (1966). His contributions are detailed in Chapter 4.

Since Mueller and Kaplan made their voices heard, much has happened. As McCarthy (1997) notes, during the 1970s and early 1980s and spearheaded by European music educators (see, for instance, Vulliamy & Lee, 1976), music educators in the United States began to pay some attention to the influence of the mass media and popular culture on musical values and behaviors of students. Although the focus on large ensemble instruction and competitive music performance in secondary schools makes it difficult to introduce popular music as a component of the curriculum, it remains of interest for general music specialists, especially when they teach students at the upper-level elementary, middle-school, and junior high levels (Hebert & Campbell, 2000; Middleton, 1990).

Another movement, derived more from ethnomusicological than music sociological thinking, has been an effort to teach multiethnic awareness by means of global music repertoire and activities. Many resource materials are available to music educators, but, as suggested in this text, the debate over multiculturalism in music education continues.

The need to learn about multicultural music making was also the impetus for Barbara Reeder Lundquist's proposal for a sociomusical research agenda for music educators (Lundquist, 1984a, 1984b). Strongly influenced by ethnomusicologist John Blacking, Lundquist argued that music teachers and researchers needed to understand the cultural and societal context of which our knowledge about music is a part. Second, music teachers and researchers should know that such knowledge is shaped by the role humans place on making and using music in particular situations.

Also beginning in the mid-1980s, several music education philosophers acknowledged the importance of social factors in an individual's musical learning. Conferences and symposia brought issues of music as "a socially significant enterprise" (Bowman, 1994, p. 64) to the fore. Music as a vehicle of social affirmation or social exclusion became a common theme in academic writings as did the assertion that musical learning is not only an educational enterprise but also a sociopolitical one. Musical taste and preference were interpreted as culture specific and contextually bound to upbringing, ethnicity, race, gender, and the conditions under which an individual is engaged with music.

An increased interest in sociological issues pertaining to music instruction can also be documented by the space allotment in the two extant handbooks of music education research, published respectively in 1992 and 2002. The first (Colwell, 1992) contains only one chapter on the sociology of music; the second handbook (Colwell & Richardson, 2002) has an entire section entitled "Social and Cultural Contexts." Edited by Marie McCarthy, its scope reflects the diverse sociological platforms by which researchers explain the social nature of music teaching and learning. It now is timely to dedicate an entire book to introducing U.S. music teachers to the pertinent relationship between sociological thinking and music instructional processes.

Introductory texts should by their nature be brief. Some informed readers might notice quickly that, with a few exceptions, the book omits references to how European music sociologists and scholars have articulated and researched the connection between sociology and music education. This omission, although regrettable, is deliberate because of the different instructional realities Europeans face. As valuable as many of the European sources are that describe both music and educational issues from a sociological perspective, they would require extensive background information before data and findings could be meaningfully compared to circumstances music teachers encounter in the Americas and, specifically, in the United States.

1

The Performer and Teacher in You

A Matter of Identity

Live in tune.

Introduction

A sociology of practical value for music teachers should begin with each teacher as an individual, how she has become who she is; how he interacts with others around him—whether in personal face-to face interactions or interactions through the Internet. Such self-knowledge becomes relevant when trying to understand why our students do not necessarily think like we do or why they act in ways foreign to our own thinking. Being aware of the origins of our own thinking about music and education also can clarify why others around us, school administrators, our students' parents, and the school community, often attach different values to music and the arts in society than we, the music teachers, do.

Especially in music as a required subject, the value systems of music teachers and students tend to be at odds with each other. The reasons are many and have been addressed by, for example, Farnsworth (1969) and North, Hargreaves, and Tarrant (2002). Sociological studies suggest that, given the social makeup of to-day's society, which is multiethnic, multiracial, and socially diverse, chances are high that the seeming disconnect between school music culture and everyday culture will continue to be a force with which music teachers have to reckon.

Charles Fowler picked up on this fact when, in 1991, he foresaw "troubled waters" for music education in several ways. One such way was the documented waning of public support for the arts, at least as classically trained artists define the arts. This trend continues today and makes Fowler's statement that "the troubled waters of music education make the need for new concepts imperative" (1991, p. 3) even timelier than when it was written.

One of those new and imperative concepts may be that music teachers learn to trace and understand their own role in the instructional process from a sociological perspective. Examining our social roots can teach us about ourselves as the musicians, teachers, or students we are. We not only understand our own identity but may also be able to discern social and cultural differences between ourselves and those with whom we work every day, be they our students, their parents, our school administrators, music peers, or our nonmusician colleagues.

Communicating with each of these groups becomes a conscious act of considering why we, the teachers, act the way we do; who our students are; and how they and we fit into the school community at large. The student's question, "Why can't we ever sing *good* songs?" can be interpreted more accurately if we have taken time to learn about the student's social identity, especially as it is still evolving, and compare it to our own at the time we were the student's age.

When we articulate our socioeconomic and cultural background for the purpose of getting a sense of our own position in society as compared to that of others around us, we describe our **socialization (D)**. Beginning with infancy and continuing well into our adult lives, our socialization is about who we are at any given point in our lives and what social and cultural forces have impacted us.

Sociologists have divided these processes into phases, all of which are interrelated. **Primary socialization (D)** occurs earliest, usually much controlled by those closest to us, parents, guardians, or other primary caregivers. **Secondary socialization (D)** generally begins as we enter school, be it preschool or kindergarten, and is usually assumed to last throughout our high school years. Then, as we make decisions about our professional goals and education, the tertiary phase of socialization begins, also referred to as a person's **occupational socialization (D)**. Later chapters explain all of these processes in greater detail. Taking into consideration the close connection between all socialization phases, this chapter focuses on aspects imbedded in what sociologists call **occupational identity (D)**.

In 2002, social psychologists MacDonald, Hargreaves, and Miell (2002) published *Musical Identities*. The term as used in their book describes the relationship of an individual to music and the impact that relationship has on the individual's *personal* development. The term *occupational identity* as used in this chapter in reference to musicians describes the view that working musicians have constructed of themselves as participants in the workforce.

Small Group Discussion 1.1

Introduce yourselves to each other and talk about your respective family, musical, and educational backgrounds. Touch on experiences inside and outside of school that you believe had a bearing on your choice of studying music and/or becoming a music teacher.

Occupational Identities in Music

Musicians know well the close connection between early involvement in the making of music and the choices that eventually led to their decision to pursue music professionally. They remember the impact of family members, teachers, and peers on those decisions, and they can recall what got them so engaged in music that they chose to study music professionally.

University students in preparation for becoming music teachers are at the beginning of developing such an identity through the work they do as aspiring musicians and music education majors. Applied lessons, the ensembles in which they participate, and any or all of the other music courses not only advance their musical skills and knowledge but also the image of themselves as musicians and, possibly, future music teachers.

Commonly, the image trained musicians have of themselves is that of a professional performer. However, the image of music teacher can emerge as well even though it may be overshadowed by one's desire to fit into the community of musicians that music schools typically represent. It therefore is quite natural that, courses in education and pedagogy notwithstanding, music education students are often more engaged in thinking about themselves as aspiring professional performers than as future school music teachers.

Once a school employee, one of the best ways to determine how you see yourself professionally is to listen to your answer when someone asks you what you do for a living. Do you say you are a teacher? Musician? Music teacher? Music educator? More importantly, do those terms mean different things to you? If so, what are they? When you are in charge of a beginner woodwind class in middle school, do you see yourself in the role of conductor, teacher, or both?

Next to being aware of the label you give yourself, are you a dues-paying member of one or more professional associations? As a student, are you an active member of your local student organization? If you consider yourself a performer first and foremost, are you a member of good standing in the musicians' union? As a music teacher, do you hold a membership in, among others, your state music education organization?

In addition to organizational memberships at the state and national level, music teachers may also be members of the Organization of American Kodály Educators, the Music Teachers National Association, the American Choral Directors Association, the American Band Directors Association, and/or the National Jazz Educators Association. With the exception, where they exist, of local teacher unions, membership by music teachers in purely educational organizations, such as (in the United States) the National Educational Association (NEA) or the American Educational Research Association (AERA), is surprisingly rare. At times, teachers join such organizations for what may be called political reasons: One considers it wise to be part of a particular group because colleagues expect it and it reflects well on one's résumé.

At present, few data exist on the memberships in the various professional organizations to which individual school music teachers belong. It also is not clear how many members are actively involved in the policies and programs of the organizations/associations at the local, state, and/or national level. The fact that comparatively few music teachers join purely educational organizations indicates a strong allegiance of music teachers to their subject matter. Their musician identity outweighs their identity as an aspiring educator.

Early Identity Research on Musicians

The term *identity* is useful when describing how we see ourselves in relationship to other people, both personally and in the workforce. Sociologists have spent a great deal of time on this subject, and I go into greater detail about it later in the book. If you would like an explanation and definition of the term in its relationship to occupational socialization at this point, refer to Brian Roberts's (2004) online article, "Who Is in the Mirror?"[1]

How do musicians see themselves as artists and members of a workforce? Research on these and related questions has been conducted in the past by a number of general sociologists with interest in music (e.g., Becker, 1976, 1982; Coffman, 1971; Etzkorn, 1966; Faulkner, 1971, 1973; Frederickson & Rooney, 1988; Kamerman & Martorella, 1983; Kealy, 1974, 1980; McCall & Simmons, 1978) as well as musicians interested in sociology (e.g., Nash, 1954, 1957, 1961; Stebbins, 1964, 1966). The studies include research on the identities of freelance musicians and jazz band musicians, symphony musicians, studio musicians, songwriters, and composers.

Examined were (1) how musicians acquired norms and values that contributed to their occupational belief systems, and (2) how working musicians upheld and honed the musical skills and knowledge they deemed most important in their work. The studies also describe the career commitment of working musicians in terms of career achievements and other rewards. Finally, the studies explain how musicians formed occupational allegiances through formal and informal contacts.

Often as the result of long-term observations of musicians at work, researchers reported how musicians viewed their own role and status in the organizations that hired them, their relationship to other members in the ensemble and the conductor or bandleader, and what it meant to be a hired hand in the music world. The studies talk about expectations of artistic and creative independence on the one hand and experiences as servants and replaceable numbers on the other. Issues of alienation in the workplace and burnout were frequently cited, and the researchers pointed to the power of institutions on each member's personal and artistic liberties.

The Aspiring Music Teacher

Students preparing to become musicians generally want the autonomy associated with private studio teaching and being a freelance artist. But they also envision financial security that comes from being employed full time, with full benefits and

---

[1] http://www.siue.edu/MUSIC/ACTPAPERS/v3/Roberts04b.htm.

a pension plan that only large public or private schools can afford. These some-what mutually exclusive objectives are seemingly combined when students choose to pursue a music education degree that includes public school teaching certification. It is a compromise that often pleases a student's parents more than the student.

Perhaps you are one of those music education students or novice teachers who chose music education for the reasons just described. Being competent as a per-former, you go to school during the day, hold a part-time job that pays your bills, and play gigs at night that make it possible to earn some extra income and get your foot into the door of professional music making. There seems to be no rea-son why the situation should change once you graduate, except that *going* to school is to be replaced by *teaching* school. You hope to have only musically tal-ented pupils who are as serious about their music study as you were about yours.

Then you receive your degree and teaching certificate and find your first full-time employment as a music teacher. You may soon discover that teaching in a public or private school is a full-time job that makes it difficult to practice and get ready for the demands of well-paying night and weekend gigs. You may also learn that not all of your students are as devoted to the study of music as you were at their age and that your work schedule as a teacher and music director requires a 12-hour or more commitment per day. Perhaps you also want to get married and have a family life. In short, you have to make adjustments to your ideals and pro-fessional dreams.

Depending on a variety of factors, the process of making those adjustments can be easy or difficult. All factors have to do with the origins of (1) the view you have of yourself as an aspiring musician, (2) how your training either has reinforced or thwarted your personal and musical hopes and dreams, and (3) how the people you associate with most closely respond to you and your career progress.

For example, a student enters the freshman year with the unfaltering expecta-tion of becoming a full-time school music teacher. Keeping that goal clearly in mind throughout all formal studies, the needed adjustments required as a first-year teacher are likely less difficult than they would be for a student whose career dreams were to be a professional conductor working only with well-trained musi-cians. If someone with such dreams began to teach as a young assistant band di-rector in charge of beginning woodwind and brass classes, dream and reality would be so far apart that coping with reconciling them would indeed pose a chal-lenge. If, in addition, the young music teacher's spouse objected to the long work hours and highly stressed demeanor when coming home, thoughts about finding a 9-to-5 job might look ever more appealing.

Some Basic Facts About Music Teaching as a Career

Job descriptions and workplaces for public school music teachers and profes-sional performers differ substantially. A certified public school music teacher works full time as an employee in an institutional setting. Most professional performers, with the exception of those who have contracts with major orchestras or with the military, are either self-employed or work part time.

A report titled *The Changing Nature of Work. Implications for Occupational Analysis* was published jointly by the Committee on Techniques for the Enhancement of Human Performance: Occupational Analysis and the Commission on Behavioral and Social Sciences and Education National Research Council (1999). In the report, teachers and musicians are categorized under professional specialty. Within that category, musicians are listed together with "writers, artists, and entertainers" and teachers are grouped together with librarians and counselors. One category suggests artists who work by themselves; the second category implies individuals working as staff members. Teachers, along with doctors and lawyers, are also described as carrying out "interactive-emotion work" (p. 156). No teacher group, including that of music teacher, is singled out by specialty area.

In the area of "interactive-emotion work," the reporting committees expect an expansion of professional and technical work in the future and predict that, to meet future contextual changes, the expansion will "necessitate . . . an even larger proportion of . . . effective interpersonal skills" (p. 157). The workforce in general will become "more diverse with respect to gender, race, education, and immigrant status" (p. 3); the boundaries between "who performs which jobs" will get softer; and "the employment outcomes and experiences of individuals working in different occupations" will become "more fluid." The report concludes that categorizing people according to the work they do will become increasingly more difficult because work changes more rapidly and takes on different requirements. The report does envision, however, that professionals, including teachers, will continue to enjoy a certain degree of autonomy in decision making.

When, as is the case in many U.S. states, alternative certification has become a reality (Feistritzer, 2001) and training as a performing artist is sufficient for certification as a school music teacher, then the predictions become reality. The boundaries between the qualifications of a professional performer and of a music teacher become blurred and their occupational identities as musicians intertwined.

However, the report may be a bit too optimistic about the future of workers in interactive-emotive occupations as decision makers. At least in the case of school music teachers, we might need to differentiate between decision makers as (1) moral guides and "music coaches" in the lives of students, and (2) decision makers as staff members in the hierarchy of the workforce.

The degree to which music teachers are as comfortable in their role as musician-performer as they are in their role as members of the general teaching staff depends on the musical and educational values they hold and where and when they developed them. It is the active involvement in music during one's earlier years both at home and in school that motivates one to become a musician. Decisions to work toward teacher certification typically occur in most cases until or shortly before entering college, sometimes even after almost all music course work has been completed.

Since the 1950s, both communities, that of professional musician and that of school (music) teacher, have tended to originate from upward-bound social classes, not the upper classes (e.g., Becker, 1951/1980; Bowles & Gintis, 1976; Lortie, 1975/2002; Pavalko, 1972a). The 1960s and 1970s saw a brief change in that regard as young people wanted to contribute in tangible ways to the betterment of society. In 1996, however, Feistritzer reported that the teaching profession consisted primarily of middle-class white women, similar to how it had been reported by Pavalko in the 1970s. But as of 2002 and contrary to their 1996 report, Feistritzer and Chester (2001) documented that, more recently, male professionals have begun to seek employment as teachers, often after having completed their military career.

Regarding the study of music, families of the affluent upper- class and the "top out-of-sight" class (Fussel, 1983, p. 16) generally consider it an appropriate activity for leisure pursuits of children and young adults but not usually as a serious career choice (see, for example, Stewart, 1992). Thus, although it is socially and academically advantaged students who enroll in music performance classes in high school, they are not necessarily encouraged by their families to continue their studies on a professional level.

Things are somewhat different among lower socioeconomic classes. Here the possibility of becoming a schoolteacher continues to be considered an upward-bound occupational choice. However, enrolling in music for serious study is perceived as a frill, a fact confirmed by Stewart's (1992) findings according to which minority and less affluent students are unlikely to participate in top high school music ensembles. The serious study of music as a part of becoming a teacher often lies outside the experience of families whose members, because of financial and other pressures, need to become a part of the workforce as quickly as possible. Thus, although the occupation of teaching is considered a secure and stable profession, the choice of music as the subject matter to be taught is often out of the question.

Small Group Discussion 1.2

Discuss your memories of classmates who participated in the same high school ensemble(s) you took part in but who made it very clear that going into music professionally was "not for them." Try to recall their reasons and how you reacted to them at the time.

The Occupational Socialization of Music Students

In 1969, Charles Kadushin described what he called the professional self-concept of undergraduate performance majors of the Manhattan School of Music and the Juilliard School of Music. Kadushin used the term *professional* to indicate an individual wanting to perform, not teach, for a living. Becoming a member of the musicians' union, getting paid for one's work, and the winning of competitions were the deciding factors for seeing oneself as a member of the occupation "professional musician" (Kadushin 1969).

Even though many of the students interviewed by Kadushin may eventually have become music teachers, neither the Manhattan nor the Juilliard School of Music has music education programs leading to teacher certification. Therefore, the students' identity as musicians was clearly shaped by norms held by professional performers.

Surprisingly, however, later studies on the occupational identity specifically of music education majors yielded similar results. The first such study (L'Roy, 1983) was a dissertation conducted at the University of North Texas (then North Texas State University). Subsequently, Brian Roberts (1991a, 1991b, 1993) published three monographs based on a pan-Canadian study of the occupational identity of music education students at five Canadian university schools of music.

Roberts' extensive findings confirmed those reported by L'Roy. Music education majors showed a strong allegiance with full-time performers, and their identity as future music teachers/educators remained weak. L'Roy's findings were somewhat surprising in that regard because the students who had responded to her questionnaire and those she had interviewed had already taken almost all of their courses in education, including those in music education. Exposure to knowledge about instructional processes apparently did not contribute to a stronger sense of self as a teacher. In fact, L'Roy commented that there seemed to be a decline in the subjects' identity as music teachers in favor of that of performer. Only those students who had gone through their student teaching experience responded with a greater sensitivity toward issues concerning instructional skills and working with students.

Roberts (1993) interpreted his findings as being all about the label of musician, rarely about the label of educator. At issue here is not that music students should not view themselves as musicians; after all, that is what they set out to become. Rather, one should note music education majors' weak affiliation with the world of education even though it is the world in which their work will take place.

Unquestionably, from the standpoint of developing a strong sense as a musician, being immersed in the study of music rather than the study of education is necessary. In the United States and Canada, the training environment of a school of music or conservatory therefore is a positive force in determining music education students' primary allegiance.

Of concern to those in charge of music teacher training programs should be music education students' weak allegiance to education as a world that one day will shape their daily work. Another concern should be that, although music teachers may continue to think of themselves as professional musicians, professional performers do not necessarily think of music teachers as "one of theirs."

Sociologically, the two worlds of work, professional performer and public school music teacher, are somewhat at odds with each other. Presently, therefore, the boundaries between the two occupations may not be as fluid as the 1999 report on the changing nature of work might have predicted.

Furthermore, musicians certified as public school teachers and working as school employees move from what they believe to be a relatively homogenous "family" of well-trained musicians into a school system with diverse interest groups. In it, music and the other arts play but a small part.

If being comfortable with and understanding multiple sets of values is the sign of a well-adjusted music teacher, then even the best preparation in the subject matter alone cannot achieve such a goal. Therefore, going through a certification process after several years of intense music study or receiving alternative certification as an accomplished performer may not be sufficient for preparing a musician adequately for what public school music teachers are expected to do.

Aware of this fact, some music schools and conservatories have begun to involve music education majors throughout their formal studies in a more immediate and direct contact with public school music programs through immersion in field experiences and teaching practica. Ongoing contacts with pupils and full-time teaching staff in the classroom are expected, prior to student teaching, to make music education students emulate the demeanors and behaviors common among all school teaching staff members. It is a model that medical schools and nursing schools, among others, have explored and debated for quite some time. It remains to be seen whether similar efforts strengthen music education majors' sense of self as educators while also maintaining their identity as musicians.

The success of immersion programs may actually depend on the students' upbringing in music and the strength of the institutions of which the students are a part. In that regard, music schools and conservatories as "insider communities" (Roberts, 1991a, p. 32) have the "upper hand" over schools of education.

Not only do music majors experience the intimacy of one-on-one instruction throughout the entirety of their music training, but they also work together in large ensembles as a musical body dedicated to a common goal of music making. Both social situations, the studio lesson and the ensemble, function as powerful socializing agents. Colleges of education have little to offer in comparative power and strength. The classes and occasional labs do not allow for one-on-one mentoring processes similar to those provided by studio teachers. And there is nothing comparable to the large ensemble that unites students as a close-knit, albeit hierarchically structured, music group.

The power of such a group is indeed strong. Its members generally accept the focus on the music performed in those ensembles even if their own preferred style may include "rock, heavy metal, country or barbershopping" (Roberts, 1991a, p. 63). As so-called systems of enculturation, schools of music affirm and strengthen students' affiliation and identification with the values espoused by the schools' faculty who serve as gatekeepers of those values (Roberts, 1991a, 2000). Spending time in the practice room is a more tangible sign of belonging to the community of musicians than is sitting in the library reading about educational policies or curriculum theories.

Similarly, when music teachers seek certification in music teaching methodologies associated with Orff and/or Kodály, their identification as musicians is stressed more than their identification as teachers. This is another indication of the power of music as a socializing agent in the work a music teacher does. The focus on the subject matter overrides the concerns that shape the world of education.

Writing Project 1.1

Do the research findings on the worlds of music teachers and professional performers just described resonate with your own experiences? If so, to what extent? If not, how do your own experiences differ?

Communities of Practice

In 2002, I suggested, "Both communities, that of musicians and that of teachers, have their own expectations of what is important, and both communities have different means to signify those expectations" (Froehlich, 2002, p. 150). Today, replacing the word *musician* with that of *professional performer* and that of *teacher* with *professional educator,* the statement still stands. The worlds of professional performance and public school music teaching are **communities of practice (D).**

Each occupation represents a community of practice. It is a real or imaginary place "where skills are acquired, rehearsed, and given value" (English National Board for Nursing, Midwifery and Health Visiting, 2000, n.p.; see also Nielsen, 1999). What are the values music teachers hold as members in a community of practice?

In his study, "The Professional Role and Status of the School Music Teacher in American Society," Howard White (1964, 1967) found that band and choral directors identified more with their performance areas than with the community of music educators as a whole. Elementary general music specialists frequently expressed that they felt they had more in common with classroom teachers than with their music colleagues at the secondary level. Even today, both findings, although dated, support the notion of separate communities of practice among musician-teachers.

From the early to mid-1990s on, several studies further explored the seeming dichotomy of teacher role vis-à-vis that of artist/performer (e.g., Bouije, 1998, 2000; Clinton, 1997; Mark, 1998; Stephens, 1993) and the status music teachers attached to their work. The findings generally concur that school music teachers do not have strong self-images of themselves as educational staff members. Also, when Bouije compared the responses of newly graduated Swedish music teachers with their responses seven years later, the perceived status of the music teaching profession actually declined in the respondents' view with increasing teaching experience.

Such findings may be typical of teachers responsible for required general music classes. Head band and choral directors in the United States who are in charge of student recruitment and fund-raising projects for their programs face realities that are most likely unfamiliar to most school music teachers in Sweden or elsewhere in Europe.

Ultimately, attempts to dichotomize a teacher's allegiance as being connected to the world of education or the world of music may be insufficient to describe music teachers' identification with their work. Instead, data may confirm public school music teachers to be members of a community of practice uniquely their own (Clinton, 1997), which itself is divided into several subcommunities with, again, different practices.

School Music Teachers' Multiple Identities

By sharing instructional choices and values with music colleagues from different schools, a community of music teachers emerges that matches neither the communities of non-music-teaching staff nor the communities of professional performers outside of schools. Such a possibility was suggested by White as early as 1964 and continues to be plausible today in light of the diversity of work music teachers do. As job requirements and teaching situations vary, so do the actions that are informed by the norms and values governing each of these settings.

To illustrate this observation, I describe music teachers' occupational status as determined by the extent to which music teachers control their own clientele and make instructional and curricular decisions without supervision. As I show in Chapter 2 of the book, these are some of the criteria by which sociologists determine the level of professional independence that governs a person's work. But how music teachers carry out these occupational obligations is also a reflection of their socialization processes, both at the personal level and as musicians and pedagogues.

Choosing the Clientele

The clientele of teachers is not only their pupils but also the pupils' parents or guardians. As one considers the autonomy music teachers have in selecting their clientele, there is a clear difference between elementary general music specialists and secondary-level music directors. Elementary general music specialists work with *all* pupils. The teacher does not choose the clientele and therefore has less autonomy in decision making than a colleague at the secondary level who teaches music as an elective.

At the secondary level of music instruction, at least two different work situations emerge. In the first one, the teacher is in charge of the top ensembles, the musical elite. It consists of students who have been selected by the teacher through an auditioning process. The teacher has musical autonomy in selecting the clientele. The second situation is one where the teacher is in charge of music electives that serve a more general student body. In this case, even though music is an elective (often called "general music"), the teacher does not choose the student body. The students are there and must be taught.

All three situations have ramifications for the way a music teacher works with the students and their parents. It is here where knowledge of the different identities in the student body becomes paramount because such knowledge can become a positive tool for maintaining classroom control.

The elementary general music specialist works with the most socially diverse student and parental body. This fact is mediated by the type of neighborhood in which a school is located but it nonetheless requires from the teacher the ability to respond on a daily basis to the needs and wishes of individuals from different socioeconomic and cultural backgrounds. Most immediately, those backgrounds play a part in a student's music preferences, knowledge of how to learn, and attitude toward school in general. General music teachers need to respond to such attitudes and social predispositions by choosing repertoire and activities that are appealing to as many students as possible, always being aware that they may not reach everybody. The same is true for junior or senior high school music teachers who teach general music as an elective, are in charge of nonauditioned ensembles in school, or teach in inner-city schools.

Head music teachers, responsible for the top performers in high school, face different challenges. One such challenge lies in understanding why some parents do not wish to see their children continue in music during high school even though they are some of the finest music students in the ensemble. Instead, the parents want their children to concentrate on academic classes in preparation for entering the best colleges in the country. Music teachers, usually coming from a different socioeconomic and educational background than their students' parents, often do not understand such a choice.

Finally, the parents of students who take music as an elective but are not driven to excel in music require yet another communicative approach. Unless they, the parents, are musically inclined as well, they are likely to show little interest in their children's progress in music. A student missing a rehearsal or even a concert has little intrinsic meaning to these parents. The same is true for the music teacher's ongoing efforts to hold parents responsible for supervising their offspring's home practice.

Teachers generally are faulted for not being well prepared to teach in schools whose populations are different from their own socioeconomic and cultural background (see, among others, Olmedo, 1997; Taylor & Sobel, 2001; Wiggins & Follow, 1999). There are presently no data to suggest this is true for music teachers as well. However, a general sensitivity about the origins of differences in attitudes, demeanors, and values toward serious music study in school can go a long way to improve our communication and teaching skills. Thus, rather than expecting that all students are similarly enthralled by the singing of a 15th-century madrigal, the teacher might not only have the students articulate their reasons for liking and disliking a style of music, but she may actually show an understanding for such reasons. As a result, she restrains from any indication, verbally or nonverbally, that she favors those students who spoke positively about such music.

Making Instructional and Curricular Decisions

If the predictions in the report on the changing nature of work prove accurate, the teachers who do "interactive-emotion work" will continue to make autonomous decisions. At the same time, however, teachers will also come from more diverse ethnic and racial backgrounds than has been the case. Also, if Feistritzer and Chester (2001) are correct, the teaching profession will see more men entering the workforce, a positive development in light of the fact that the profession needs male role models for the male student population, both in general education and in music.

Finally, if a greater diversity in the teacher body's ethnicity, gender, and race appears to be the trend of the future, the formation of more rather than fewer subgroups among teachers will be the result. Presently, it is not clear whether the same prediction holds true for music teachers. Assuming, however, that future music teachers, too, are likely to come from a wider array of ethnic and racial backgrounds than is common today, their own, more diverse personal and musical backgrounds will likely impact the success of their musical training and, thus, their work as teachers. It also means that music teachers of tomorrow might bring to their training and to their interactions with their pupils new predilections for musical styles and genres. Thus, equipped with highly developed musical skills and knowledge, they may also bring a greater sense of sensitivity and empathy to students whose primary socialization led them to different musical predilections and preferences than those the musical traditions of music schools advocate.

We might consider such a prediction positive for music in the schools. When we "think sociologically on the ground of our experience" (Agger, 2004, p. 7), each of us interacts "the way we are" with many different political, school, and music communities at the same time. The more diverse the backgrounds are that music teachers bring to the workplace "school," the more likely it is that they can reach students musically who have not been reached in the past.

As instructional staff members, music teachers are held to the cultural traditions and educational policies that shape education as a societal mandate. As such, music teachers serve as ambassadors for prevailing educational *and* musical norms and values in society. They are in charge of *transmitting* agreed-upon societal values from one generation to the next.

The question sociologists of education have raised is whether schools also *transform* extant societal values. Asked differently, is the purpose of formal education to make individuals conform to societal values or can educators contribute to freeing an individual's mind from accepted modes of thinking? Most importantly, is such a freedom needed for advancing the well-being of society at large?

The same questions exist for music teachers and their role as transmitters versus transformers of musical and cultural norms and values prevalent in society: Is the purpose of school music instruction to pass on the cultural values of past generations for the purpose of preserving what is considered today's cultural heritage, or is the purpose to prepare tomorrow's generations for engaging in music making

---

Writing Project 1.2

Following the class discussion, outline some questions you would ask selected classmates and/or other music teachers you know about their own (music) socialization processes.

---

and listening as lifelong pursuits? If the answer lies in seeking to strike a balance between both goals, how can teachers best negotiate and work with what they know and what makes up their students' music worlds?

Later chapters show sociological thinking to be pivotal in the debate of how both educational and musical values come about. It is for this reason that thinking about music teaching from a sociological perspective requires attention to music sociology as well as the sociology of education.

Questions for Class Discussion

1. How did your family react when you said you wanted to become a music teacher? Can you explain such reactions if you consider your family members' personal and professional socialization processes?

2. Describe your own socialization processes as they pertain to your education and schooling, music included. To whom do you attribute the greatest influences, positive and negative, and how would you describe the relative importance of those influences on how you see yourself today?

3. How did you decide to embark on a career in music? At which point did you become a music education major? How do you expect that decision to impact your original career plans?

2

Teaching as Work
What Educational Sociologists Tell Us

Negotiate for shared meaning.

Introduction

Historically, the professional training of future teachers has focused on methods of teaching more than on preparing them for the complexity of schools in the hierarchy of the entire educational system. From the early years of public education until roughly the middle of the 20th century, such focus was justified because schools were relatively small and connected to neighborhoods in which teachers and students knew each other outside of school.

Schools had a small instructional staff with multiple duties and a lower level of administrative as well as bureaucratic oversight than is common today. Knowledge of social classes in society was mostly a matter of academic rather than personal experience because neighborhoods were largely homogeneous. Communities of different social status and ethnic origin were geographically and politically segregated. Decision makers were not held to respond to concerns of minorities, migrant workers, and women.

Since the middle of the 20th century, this situation has changed. No longer is it sufficient to think in terms of rich and poor alone. Rather, society has become more open to acknowledging the impact of different socialization processes as significant challenges in upholding the democratic principle of seeking equal access to education and learning for all citizens. This openness comes with a cost, both for society at large and for each individual.

Specific to education, efforts to document equal access to school learning by all citizens have resulted in a much larger bureaucracy of administrative accountability than has been the case ever before. For teachers at all levels of instruction and for all subject matter areas, institutional bureaucratization demands compliance with recommendations and directives from professional associations, teacher unions, and/or state educational reform agencies. They become added objectives that have to be met in addition to all instructional objectives and, in the eyes of many teachers today, meeting such *institutional* objectives takes time away from "real teaching."

When *institutional* objectives seem to become more important than *instructional* objectives, the act of teaching itself appears to be devalued. This is what novice teachers experience almost as soon as they enter the workforce. They learn that in addition to being "king in the classroom" or, as is the case for music teachers, "boss on the podium," they also are staff members in a complex system, governed by what is institutionally possible, allowed, and considered in line with school policies and regulations. Adjustments are needed in the conception of one's envisioned work.

Learning to adjust to the hierarchy of decision-making power in any workforce is part and parcel of a person's **occupational socialization (D).** The term denotes how adults perceive their role in the workplace from day one until they retire and how those roles are perceived by others around them.

This chapter describes some of the characteristics that fall under the rather broad concept of occupational socialization. Wherever feasible, I also refer to general job characteristics of school music teachers to show differences and similarities between nonmusic instructional staff members and school music staff. A section on a few prototypical studies in the field of education follows, providing some early sociological data that remains of interest. The chapter concludes with a discussion of the relationship between a teacher's occupational identity as pedagogue and subject matter expert.

The Concept of Occupational Socialization

Some older literature in sociology, namely from the 1970s and 1980s, has examined what makes a profession different from a labor and a semiprofession different from a profession (see, for example, Abbott, 1988; Becker, 1970/1977; Freidson, 1986; Pavalko, 1971, 1972b; Simpson, 1972). The differences are generally believed to lie in the degree of autonomy of decision making associated with the type of work one does as well as the freedom one has in choosing one's clientele and determining one's fee structure.

If Becker called the debate "old" in 1970, it certainly continues to be unresolved even today. At present, the consensus among sociologists seems to be to use the term *occupation* as a "value-free" descriptor of what a person does for a living. Because as occupations change, so may their descriptors and the values attached to them (Bowe, Bowe, & Streeter, with Murphy & Kernochan, 2000; Engvall, 1997; Erikson & Vallas, 1990).

Becker (1970/1977) suggests that the term *professional* is in reality "an honorific title" (p. 93) because members in the occupation as well as laypersons need to *believe* that these sets of ideas are present even if they are not. For example, doctors, lawyers, and accountants are generally perceived by the public to have autonomy as professionals. Seemingly in control of choosing their clientele and determining their fee structure, doctors and lawyers as well as independent certified public accountants (CPAs) supervise their own work, be it through the American Bar Association, the American Medical Association, or the CPA Accrediting Agency. All three are peer-elected professional associations.

As doctors join health maintenance organizations, lawyers ever-larger law firms, and CPAs large financial institutions, professional autonomy is lessened. Clients are assigned rather than chosen, and the supervisory control shifts from the self-governed board to a much more complex bureaucratic system of hierarchically tiered power relationships. This type of work comes close to what is referred to as a semiprofession.

Nurses and social workers are believed to be semiprofessionals. They still have specialized skills that they apply in relative freedom from supervision, but their clientele is assigned to them and they work under a predetermined fee structure, especially if they work in a hospital or larger institutional settings. In contrast to semiprofessionals, laborers' work allows little to no personal decision making. The tasks are assigned, routinized, and under the control of the worker's immediate supervisor. Fee structures are negotiated between labor unions and the employers.

Where does school teaching as an occupation fit in this three-leveled hierarchy of decision-making power? Is it a profession akin to that of what doctors and lawyers do, a service like that provided in relative autonomy by nurses and social workers, or a labor similar to what assembly-line workers do? Finally, is it unified enough across subject matters and function that one category suffices to describe the work teachers do? This chapter answers these questions relative to various job descriptions of school music teachers.

Teacher unions, where they exist, have worked for decades to "professionalize" teaching mainly by arguing for better pay and benefit packages and seeking more negotiating power for the teacher unions themselves. Music teachers are included in those negotiations.

As professional associations and educational foundations strive for greater control over how teachers are trained, teacher preparation programs have more stringent subject matter requirements than ever before. Novice teachers are placed in state and privately funded professional development learning centers where experienced mentors guide the inexperienced teachers. At the same time, though, school boards and districts rely increasingly on alternative certification for experienced subject matter experts, such as professional performers, who generally have little to no pedagogical expertise.

Such facts send conflicting messages to the teaching profession regarding the relative value of subject matter knowledge vis-à-vis professionally developed pedagogical experience. What appears as a positive development on the one hand, namely stricter enforcement of both pedagogical and subject matter knowledge, is downplayed when subject matter experts can enter the classroom without pedagogical expertise. The training phase specific to teacher preparation is devalued. Ultimately, therefore, the professionalism of teachers does not appear to lie in their pedagogical expertise but in the substance of their subject matter knowledge. This applies both to teachers in general and music teachers in particular.

Indeed, if professionalism means independent decision making based on subject matter knowledge, most school music teachers are professionals. Very few school districts dictate whether students are to be taught music according to principles espoused bv Orff, Kodály, or according to other music-philosophical trends. Ensemble directors at the secondary level, too, are relatively free of music-specific guidelines by which they are evaluated. Rather, they are expected to comply with the same instructional standards of teaching effectiveness by which their nonmusic colleagues are evaluated.

Musically, music teachers are autonomous, with the exception, of course, that the school concerts be pleasing to the parents and the general public, that the half-time shows be entertaining, and that participation in festivals and competitions be successful and reflect well on the school. These are pressures that may be comparable to those that teachers of other subject matter experience as the result of being held responsible for the outcomes of standardized student testing. There are no data currently on whether those pressures are comparable to the ones music teachers experience when they produce public performances.

When examining characteristics of an occupation from a sociological perspective, several interrelated key elements need to be considered. The ones singled out in this chapter are (1) a teacher's occupational norms and values, (2) his or her role in the workforce, (3) perceived or actual career mobility and status, and (4) commitment to the execution of specific work tasks and skills. They apply equally to the work musicians do and to what teachers do. Therefore, they certainly apply to what music teachers do.

Occupational Norms and Values

Hardly any sociological dictionary defines the terms *norm* and *value* without referring to their interdependence. **Social norms (D)** are rules or principles of behavior that define a particular social group and determine the values shared by the individuals in a group. At times, values are voluntarily shared; at other times, they are intentionally or unintentionally imposed on a group of people. The degree to which groups of people share the same values also defines the degree of similarity in their normative behaviors.

Applied to music and the arts, the values that define the normative behavior of classically trained musicians are different from those found among untrained musicians or among the public at large. Such normative behavior comes about because of traditions, conventions, and expectations that classically trained musicians embrace as theirs and pass on to newcomers. Once the musical traditions, conventions, and expectations common to the group of classically trained musicians have been accepted and become internalized by any "newcomer" to the group, the norms and values of music as an art form are embraced as well. It is a requirement to becoming an insider to the group of classically trained musicians, individuals who look at music "as an art form" first and only secondly "as a mode of expression" (Gruhn, 1999).

Not all students who enter professional music study understand this process. Still thinking of music as a mode of expression first, listening to classical master-pieces and immersing themselves in the study of music theory and history are not what many students associate with the study of music. Few of those activities likely played an important part in the student's earlier experiences with music as a "mode of expression." Becoming socialized to the role of a classically trained musician therefore means to engage in those activities that the group of classically trained musicians has established as the norms of music "as an art form."

The distinction in today's society, culture, and educational system between music as an art form and as a mode of expression is crucial in understanding why societal values about music and the arts are not necessarily the same as those shared by pro-fessionally trained musician-artists. Of course, the same phenomenon applies to un-derstanding other social groups, be they athletes, dancers, writers, painters, nurses, physicians, lawyers, accountants, or other occupational groups.

Our Social Role in the Workforce

The observation that individuals play assigned roles in the workforce originated from a theory called role theory, first articulated by Talcott Parsons (1937, 1951) and further developed by Goffman (1959/1973) and Merton (1957, 1967). Today, the concept of **social role (D)** is accepted as a basic term in all sociological theories. The concept helps explain any interactions of two or more people with each other, be it at work or at home.

Paraphrasing Mazur (2002) in his online *Dictionary of Critical Sociology*, the notion of a doctor without a patient or a professor without a student is absurd.[1] Similarly, music teachers are defined by the subject matter for which they are re-sponsible and by the expectations their students, their colleagues, and the school administrators have of them. Professional conductors are who they are because they work with accomplished (professional) performers and report to symphony boards, not school administrators. How individuals in the workforce play out their roles depends (1) on how they see each of the other "players" in the workforce carry out their roles, and (2) how the "others" see them.

If all players are familiar with the rules that govern their interactions, they share a normative culture that is defined by agreed-upon values. Such is the case for most music students who finished their formal years of study. They are at ease and familiar with the way music schools operate; they have become socialized to the values that define those settings.

Upon graduation and beginning their first teaching job, novice music teachers enter a new normative culture, the schools that have hired them. Here, music plays a lesser role in the value system because other values, such as maintaining discipline

---

[1] http://www.public.iastate.edu/~rmazur/dictionary/a.html

among the pupils, keeping pace with administrative routines, and fitting in with the rest of the teaching staff, take precedence over the values toward which the beginning music teacher had been socialized.

Different and unfamiliar role expectations lead to uncertainty of how to act. A sense of what sociologists call **role distance (D)** is the result, which often ends up in experiences of **role conflict (D)** in the workplace. Its occurrence indicates how individuals work with each other and their superiors in what outsiders may perceive as a harmonious community of like-minded individuals (Achinstein, 2002).

Career Mobility and Status

A defining characteristic of any occupation is a person's opportunity to climb the career ladder. It generally is assumed to be an upward movement that corresponds to a hierarchy of positions within the chosen occupation. This is especially true for occupations in bureaucratic organizations, such as schools.

Career mobility is imbedded in the way society is stratified according to classes and social groups, and how any one organization in society is stratified in terms of hierarchies of power. Such power expresses itself in a number of concrete, that is, verifiable, as well as merely assumed privileges. Among them are (1) monetary earnings and steady increases in those earnings, (2) promotions to higher "ranks" in the profession, (3) liberty to come and go as one pleases, (4) freedom to make decisions based on expertise, and (5) how one ranks among one's peers as indicated by mentoring roles and elected or appointed advisory positions in committees and/or associations.

Career patterns are not only defined by the position a person holds in the workplace but also by the extent to which the person, as a son or daughter, exceeds the educational and social attainment of his or her parents. This means that upward mobility in a career touches on two issues: the social positions individuals envision to hold at the peak of their careers, and the leadership positions with which they wish to be identified in their workplace.

An example relevant to music would be the middle-school ensemble teacher who moves up, as it were, to the high school ensemble when that teacher leaves. Being the head band director of a high school is viewed as a position of higher prestige (and, in some instances, financial reward) than remaining a middle-school band director. Presently, a teacher's main opportunity to move up the career ladder is to go into administration, something many band directors strive for as they see their organization and leadership skills being redeployed.

Next to work that has opportunities for upward mobility, there also are occupations characterized more by lateral career moves. This type of move in the workforce is a horizontal one because it does not result in an outwardly better social position or status than the previous one.

Some studies described in this chapter suggest that teachers appear to make horizontal moves within the same hierarchical tier more often than upward ones; in the perception of others, the individual's social status in the peer group of professionals does not change. The reasons for such moves are often personal and tied to a teacher's search for a position that promises easier working conditions, be it by reducing travel time, a better work schedule, or a seemingly easier rapport with administrators, parents, and students. More recent data also suggest that most teachers seek employment in schools similar to and preferably close to the communities from where they, the teachers, graduated. Familiarity of environment gives one a sense of easier working conditions.

Sociologically, lateral moves are considered static and therefore detrimental to opportunities for professional growth. However, not all individuals perceive lateral moves as static. Staying at the same school as the head choral director might mean more to someone than making more money in another school district. Also, becoming a mentor for less experienced teachers might serve a music teacher's need for an upward career move even though the visible reward may at best be a teaching load reduction.

Commitment to the Execution of Specific Work Tasks and Skills

The honorific title of *professional* of which Becker spoke becomes most readily seen in the way an individual shows commitment to fulfilling all work-related duties, be they self-chosen or imposed. For example, a teacher's commitment to the subject matter itself is an indicator of the professionalism referred to by Becker. As described before, that commitment is evident through membership in educational and subject matter–related organizations, volunteering for certain duties in school, and the degree of voluntary contacts with colleagues for the purpose of advancing one's own work. Such a commitment also affirms and therefore deepens the group structure of which the individual is a part.

A teacher's work is characterized not just by the act of teaching itself but also by such duties as preparing students for the taking of standardized tests, providing paper trails for all instructional actions taken, filing reports, keeping records of student learning, attending to all other bookkeeping tasks expected of today's teachers, and being observed on a regular basis for the purpose of documenting instructional excellence. Experienced teachers usually have learned to accept these tasks as integral to their job description. Novice teachers, however, consider such tasks as extraneous to their job. It is the sign of a mature professional to accept such duties as part of the work requirements. One has become fully socialized to the norms and values of the teaching profession.

Small Group Discussion 2.1

Discuss the significance of knowing your role in the workplace. Give examples that describe your experiences in various workplaces, not just necessarily school teaching.

Teachers as Staff Members in Public Schools: Selected Landmark Studies

How have teachers viewed their work in terms of the characteristics just outlined and how does the public see teachers? The studies selected for review in this section include classics in the field of sociology and education. Included are also more recent data on teacher demographics, selection, and retention provided by representatives of various educational associations and foundations.

The Nature of Institutional Work: Becker's Contributions

Howard S. Becker's research on what defines work sociologically is on teachers (1951/1980, 1952, 1970/1977), medical students (Becker, Geer, Hughes, & Strauss, 1961/1977), professional dance musicians and their audience (1963a, 1963b), and undergraduate students in academic life (Becker, Geer, & Hughes, 1968/1995). He is a prolific writer whose contributions to the sociology of education and music are legend.[2]

In his work on teachers, Becker especially paid attention to the nature of career mobility and hierarchical relationships among teachers and their students. The data stem in large part from his dissertation (Becker, 1951/1980; 1970/1977), which included sixty interviews, mostly with female teachers, and from additional field research in the 1960s and early 1970s.

When viewed from such vantage points as prestige, influence, and income, the lateral career moves alluded to earlier were clearly present in Becker's sample. Unless a teacher chose to step into an administrative role as vice principal or principal, all career moves remained in the teaching realm itself. Any improvements in the career were seen as the result of what the teachers described as wanting to teach at better schools. A better school, in their view, was determined by the social-class composition of the school population and the "presence or absence of the 'right' kind of pupils, parents, principal, and colleagues" (Becker, 1970/1977, p. 168).

Next to looking for better schools, career patterns were also characterized by a teacher wanting "to adjust to a routine of work which [was] customary, congenial, and predictable" (p. 171). It reflected a willingness to serve the cause of education. Longevity in a position led to authority with pupils, parents, and colleagues. Problems of keeping discipline with the pupils lessened, and the teacher's authority with the parents (that is, the public) increased. Settling into a position with which one was satisfied, therefore, was perceived to be more important than upward mobility.

Once a satisfactory position had been obtained, career dangers were perceived as coming only from the outside; for example, when new school administrators took over and/or socioeconomic changes in the neighborhood led to a racially and ethnically different student body. According to Becker, the student body presented the greatest danger because a changed student body meant a different relationship

---

[2] http://http://home.earthlink.net/~hsbecker/

with the public, especially the parents, and thereby also a change of social status for the teacher.

Teachers perceived students from a lower-class economic background and of different ethnicity more difficult to teach; at the same time, though, those students' parents were considered easier to deal with than parents of faster learning upper-class pupils. In general, the teachers felt that parental interference in the educational process upset "an otherwise predictable and controllable institutional structure" (Becker, 1951/1980, p. 243). The teachers believed that such interference from what usually were upper-class parents questioned their professional authority. Becker interpreted this belief as "a chronic feature of service institutions." It signifies an "indifference or ignorance of the client with regard to the authority system set up by the institutional functionaries" (Becker, 1970/1977, p. 151).

Teacher Self-Selection and Retention: Pavalko's Contributions

Like Becker, Ronald Pavalko was interested in the larger issue of what makes work what it is, particularly in such specialty areas as "industrial sociology, social stratification, and the study of complex organizations" (1971, p. 1). He was concerned with what he called the occupation-profession continuum. It is determined by a number of factors, among them the occupational choices people make and the social significance behind such choices; occupational socialization processes before, during, and after professional training; vertical and lateral career mobility (the issue to which Becker spoke as well); and the impact of the work setting and ideology on a person's experience with work alienation.

Pavalko's chapter in *Sociological Perspectives on Occupations* (1972a) describes survey data, obtained over seven years, of who actually entered the teaching profession during the late 1960s. Like Becker, he limited his sample to female teachers because he saw elementary and secondary school teaching in the United States to be a predominantly woman's occupation and also as an example of a labor force in which a person does not stay permanently.

Teacher demographics of today seem to have changed somewhat in terms of gender. But teaching is still what Pavalko called a "discontinuous labor force participation" (p. 239), especially among teachers who have taught for less than five years. Pavalko conducted the study for the purpose of examining patterns of retention and attrition in a particular type of labor force, one that requires extensive training and investment of resources but is also characterized by less than desirable career continuity. Two surveys, conducted in 1957 and 1964 respectively, showed socioeconomic background to function "as a selective factor in the recruitment of teachers" (p. 243). The women who pursued teaching as a career choice but did not stay in it were generally from higher socioeconomic backgrounds and measured higher on intelligence tests than did teachers who remained in the teaching profession; consequently, "attrition was higher among teachers of higher measured intelligence" (p. 247). As might be expected, the most contributing factor to attrition was marriage, but the data also suggest that at the time the surveys were conducted teaching as work attracted women from what now might be called the upper lower classes and the lower upper classes.

The Nature of Public School Teaching: Lortie's Contributions

Dan C. Lortie's book *Schoolteacher. A Sociological Study* (1975/2002) details historical as well as empirical approaches toward studying the nature of the public school teaching profession. In Lortie's view, too little research existed on that subject in the 1970s. He attributed the lack of research to the fact that everybody assumed to know what teachers did even though little was known about teaching as work. In the preface to the second edition (2002), Lortie reiterated his concern, observing that "education does not change at a rapid pace—the major structures in public education are much the same today as when *Schoolteacher* was written in 1975" (2002, p. vii).

Beginning with a historical review of continuity and change in the teaching profession over three centuries of American history (Chapter 1), Lortie examined in the subsequent chapters what he called the five attractors to teaching. The attractors were, in order of importance to the interviewed teachers, (1) "to work with (young) people" (2002, p. 27), (2) "opportunity for rendering important service" (p. 28), (3) wanting to stay in the school environment because they "liked school" (p. 29), (4) the material benefits of financial security (pp. 30–31), and (5) the work schedule/time compatibility (pp. 31–32).

The list of attractors resulted from the responses not only from the elementary school teachers he interviewed in 1975 but also from data obtained in a large-sample survey conducted by the National Education Association (NEA). Lortie further validated his data by comparing them to a survey conducted in Dade County, Florida, and to data reported by other researchers. I discuss Lortie's findings under the headings as he titled them.

"Recruitment and Reaffirmation"

As stated earlier, "to work with (young) people" (2002, p. 27) was at the top of the list of attractors because teaching was believed to be "a valuable service of special moral worth" (p. 28). Another major reason for teaching as a career choice was the respondents' own positive attachment to and affiliation with schooling in their secondary socialization phase.

Anecdotal evidence today suggests that both reasons, "love for (the) students" and positive memories of one's own schooling, continue to be cited by teachers as prime motivators to become and remain educators. This appears to be the case across gender and racial divides, whether one holds an inner-city teaching position or one in the suburbs.

The theme of material benefit resulted in some juxtapositions between the attitude toward service and the hesitation to be up front about issues of monetary rewards and benefits. Lortie saw "normative pressures" at work that made "it probable that material benefits influence[d] teachers' decisions more than their answers indicate[d]" (p. 30). The incentive of higher salaries usually did not enter in women's alternative career choices, nor did the female teachers find their salaries deficient. Lortie did point out, however, that "a significant proportion" of the men he interviewed came "from homes marked by economic insecurity and low social status" (p. 30).

Small Group Discussion 2.2

Describe experiences you had that might serve as examples for facing hierarchical relationships in your own schooling. What impact did those experiences have for the way you learned?

"The Limits of Socialization"

Regarding the interviewees' responses to how they had become the professionals they perceived themselves to be, Lortie distinguished between such factors as (1) formal schooling (both general and specialized), (2) mediated entry (apprenticeship and mentoring), and (3) learning-while-doing (p. 57). He found that relatively few hours were required for learning how to teach. The short "mediated entry" in the form of practice teaching at the end of a student's educational studies did little to change the teachers' view that one learned how to teach "while doing."

When it came to the teachers' specialization in subject matter skills and knowledge, however, the teachers attached significance to the training they had received prior to teaching. In fact, their commitment to those skills and knowledge was strong. Unfortunately, neither Lortie nor Becker and Pavalko identified the subject matter each teacher represented.

As far as what caused the teachers to choose their work, imitative learning proved to be a powerful source of wanting to become a teacher; so powerful, in fact, that the profession itself did not come across as having an agreed-upon "common 'memory' or technical subculture" (p. 70) to which everybody adhered in daily practice.

A regular apprenticeship as practiced in many crafts and professions is a sequenced "series of tasks of ascending difficulty" (p. 72). Neither a student's experience during practice teaching nor one's first teaching position came close to that model. Learning how to teach continued to be an intuitive, individualistic approach of selecting what appeared to work for each individual rather than what the teaching profession has established as agreed-upon strategies and behaviors.

Lortie drew these conclusions because he found that when it came to mentorship and guidance through supervisory leadership by the assistant principal or some other designated person, teachers rarely heeded such advice. They relied on themselves and on colleagues closest to their own rank to know what was effective teaching. Guidance from those in higher positions was viewed to be less important.

"Career and Work Rewards"

Income profiles between members of different professions differ greatly. In some professions, a person may begin with very little income but, with success, will gain ever-higher earnings. Lortie calls them "staged income profiles."

Staged income profiles usually go hand in hand with upward shifts in status. Unstaged profiles are those where "income gains may be steady but small" (2002, p. 82) and status remains relatively unchanged. Teaching belongs in that category. However, in some instances, a low status is actually rewarded with relatively high earnings as, for example, those of a building supervisor.

Lortie wanted to find out what teachers valued as rewards that counterbalanced their unstaged income profile and their somewhat nonstratified career mobility. In comparing teaching to the legal profession on which Lortie (1959) had reported data, he found that the absence of career stages in teaching led to tentativeness of future commitments. The result was what he called a disjunction between involvement by time and money expenditures and "satisfaction as measured by readiness to teach again" (1975/2002, p. 91). The disjunction was smallest for married female teachers and highest for males. As a result, "few beginning teachers project[ed] long futures in the classroom; men expect[ed], in the main, to leave, and women [saw] their participation as contingent" (p. 99) on personal circumstances.

Interview Project 2.1

Talk to two different music teachers whose work you admire and who you consider role models for yourself. Discuss with them how they see themselves as professionals in their workplace and how they handle possible disagreements among themselves, other nonmusic faculty members, and school administrators.

"Perspectives on Purpose, Uncertainties, Teacher Sentiments, and Interpersonal Preferences"

Interpreting the teachers' personal views about issues they faced every day, Lortie noted that the teachers identified most strongly with the students they taught and saw purpose in reaching them. This observation supports Pavalko's findings. Teachers took pride in their craft, describing successful moments of teaching even if they only talked about one student (p. 121). They saw themselves as (1) moral agents, (2) intellectual motivators/facilitators of learning, or as (3) "inclusive" teachers, findings which Lortie qualified by stating that the differences in the role perceptions "reveal value differences which retard occupational solidarity" (1975/2002, p. 115).

Among the uncertainties listed by the teachers were questions about their role as leaders and an ambiguity between wanting to be in control at the same time that they accepted and endorsed "the hegemony of the school system on which [they were] economically and functionally dependent" (p. 186). The interviewed teachers exhibited internally contradictory role perceptions that reflected dilemmas in the teacher role itself, which eventually also shaped the interactions with parents, colleagues, the principal, and the general public.

The Teaching Staff as School Personnel: Bidwell's Contributions

Two works, "Teacher Types, Workplace Controls, and the Organization of Schools" (Bidwell, Frank, & Quiroz, 1997) and "School as Context and Construction: A Social Psychological Approach to the Study of Schooling" (Bidwell, 2000), introduce Charles Bidwell's way of studying what teachers do. He and his colleagues explained teaching as work imbedded in a system of organizational control over which teachers themselves have no control. Underlying Bidwell's research is the assumption that the organizational structure impacts work control and the "teachers' conceptions of the purposes and methods of teaching and, correspondingly, their classroom practices" (Bidwell et al., 1997, p. 285).

Teacher Types and Work Control Mechanisms

In their 1997 study, Bidwell et al. hypothesized a direct link between certain types of teachers and the controls that schools exercise. The researchers developed measurement scales to portray four teacher types: *the rigorist, the moral agent, the pal,* and *the progressivist.*

A progressivist as defined by Bidwell et al. "stresses developing higher-order mental processes and intellectual independence through the use of flexible, adaptive teaching methods" (p. 289). It is a characterization similar to the teacher type Lortie called intellectual motivators/facilitators. Also, Bidwell et al.'s definition for *moral agent* comes close to what Lortie described as moral agents, and what Lortie called the inclusive teacher resembles Bidwell's definition of *the pal.*

The control mechanisms present in and defining a teacher's workplace were labeled bureaucratic, autocratic-oligarchic, market, or collegial. Related to school size and relative client power, the latter refers to the influence and/or pressure parents and students, via their parents, can exert on what schools do.

Of thirteen selected high schools in the Chicago metropolitan area, the larger schools enrolled 2,500 to 3,000 students and employed 200 to 300 teachers; the small schools enrolled 300 to 600 students and employed between 30 and 80 faculty. Regardless of school size, parents of higher socioeconomic status (SES) had greater clientele power than parents with a lower SES, meaning that parents from different socioeconomic backgrounds exercised different degrees of control over school issues. As confirmed by the principals in schools with higher SES clientele, such control even reached into curriculum issues, a domain usually believed to be controlled by the experts—the teaching staff. The connection between teachers and administrators appeared to be loose if not weak, an observation Lortie had made as well.

School as a "Museum of Virtue"

In his essay "School as Context and Construction: A Social Psychological Approach to the Study of Schooling," Bidwell (2000) suggests that the act of schooling is constrained by "firmly institutionalized curricula and by . . . conceptions of what school is that make the school a 'museum of virtue' and the teacher its curator" p. 289. He contends that too much effort has been spent on studying and fostering achievement outcomes without taking into consideration the social effects that go along with such achievement models. Teaching effectiveness may have as much to do with workplace control and the way schools are organized as with purely instructional issues. Tracking students' learning according to ability levels is one such example that determines the instructional reality of teachers responsible for required subjects in the curriculum.

Whereas elementary general music teachers are virtually free from such control mechanisms as tracking, ensemble directors have instituted it freely in the way they determine chair placement, audition procedures, and other competitive measures that characterize professional music study. It is a normative behavior in music schools and has become central to music instructional practices in the public schools. Perhaps the same holds true for this type of tracking that holds true for the tracking observed by Bidwell: It does have social and psychological consequences of which teachers should be fully aware. Key issues in what Bidwell calls a new approach toward measuring the effectiveness of schools should include (1) definitions of the roles of faculty and students in particular instructional settings; (2) the emergence, consistency, and stability of experiences that shape those roles; and (3) key organizational attributes of schools that often are highly competitive and can create conflicts in desired learning outcomes (p. 27).

Writing Project 2.1

Articulate in writing your own position on alternative certification for music teachers in light of trends to professionalize what music educators do.

Occupational Socialization and Subject Matter: The Main Source for Professionalism?

Statements by education authorities in the online magazine *Edutopia. Envision the Future of Education*[3] affirm that teaching as work must be understood so that teacher education programs can go beyond the teaching of pedagogy alone and include an explanation of "teaching as a component part of a complex social situation" (Bidwell, 2000, p. 19). Music teachers, too, can benefit from such knowledge, even if it is for the purpose of comparing their own situation to that of their nonmusic colleagues. In doing so, they may find the norms and values of the social group "music teacher" to be in some ways different from that of the social group "schoolteacher," yet in other ways quite comparable.

Today, teacher recruits come from a more diverse population than was the case during the 1970s and 1980s (Feistritzer, 2001). Instead of "young, white females who are majoring in education and coming out of schools of education," Feistritzer observes that the diversity does not only include more minority teachers but also more males, "mostly from the military" (p. 2). There are what Feistritzer calls "career switchers and . . . people . . . interested in teaching in high-demand areas of the country, such as inner cities and outlying rural areas."

As described by Becker, Pavalko, and Lortie, teachers continue to be proud of the craft of teaching and their role of what both Lortie and Bidwell called the role of moral agent. But this pride is at risk when teachers find that more than subject matter competencies are needed to do a good job. How to deal with students, their parents, and school administrative rules and regulations are not typically a part of what intern teachers learn when visiting public schools during their professional training. The social and bureaucratic complexity of the school as workplace remains hidden to them.

It appears that teachers' sense of what Becker calls the honorific title of *professional* comes from a strong sense of self in relationship to their students. But teachers also derive that same sense of professionalism from their subject matter knowledge and skills. In fact, education experts agree that subject matter knowledge is the key to good teacher preparation programs.

Such fundamental agreement among education experts may need to be qualified from a sociological perspective. This is so because, as alluded to in Chapter 1, factors that shape the subject matter area with which a teacher identifies may also contribute to the difficulties teachers have in adjusting to the school as the workplace . The norms and values typical of highly trained musicians and long developed in a music student are transplanted into the world of education, whose norms and values are familiar to music students mostly through their memories as pupils, not as staff members.

Sociologically, two worlds of work are at odds with each other. A novice music teacher is asked to negotiate the differences and similarities between the two worlds

---

[3] http://www.glef.org/php/question.php?id=Art_850&key=039

in a matter of one day to the next. This is difficult to do because although you were strongly influenced toward thinking about music during your primary as well as secondary phase of socialization, only during your professional training did you really begin to think about teaching. While you were a student you may have observed your music teachers and decided you wanted to do what they were doing, but you did so in your role as the student musician, not in the role of a staff member in a school. The subject matter, not the general craft of teaching, was familiar to you. This may explain why the teachers described by Pavalko and Lortie felt less secure in their interactions with superiors and parents than in their subject matter knowledge.

Both Becker and Pavalko saw routinization and other laborlike characteristics in the work realities the teachers described. Those findings appear to hold today, either despite or because of efforts by educational agencies and teacher unions to control what teachers do as pedagogues and instructional staff members.

There seems to be a difference in the way teachers wish for autonomy in the classroom but also appear to submit readily to the controls of their superiors. The difference can be related to the teacher's subject matter, grade level of instruction, and gender. Music teachers at all levels of instruction, because of their close association with the subject matter, pride themselves as being knowledgeable experts in and of music. They often engage in music making outside of their work and affirm their role as musicians that way, an avenue not often available, for example, to elementary classroom teachers.

Overall, the findings are clear: Teachers' reported strong self-reliance and their unwillingness to interact closely with their administrators would imply a sense of independence that does not fit into the hierarchy of schools as they exist today. Conversely, there is compliance with imposed rules that would suggest teaching to be a semiprofessional field. Music teachers, especially ensemble directors at the secondary level, are the most peripheral to administrative controls other than those they impose on themselves. Of course, such activities as fund-raising, building strong booster clubs, and making the music program visible in the community are attributable to the fact that schools have not accepted music as an integral and fully funded part of the curriculum. Music directors must become entrepreneurial to succeed.

A relatively new issue has sprung up with the so-called site-based schools. Here the principal rather than the district determines, often with the help of a teachers' council, the instructional priorities within the school. In that case, the apparent outsider role of the music staff may hurt rather than help what music teachers try to do. Therefore, the line is fine between openly displaying one's difference as a staff member and submitting oneself willingly to curricular and administrative restraints imposed by nonmusic staff members.

In summary, it is interesting to note that sociologists and other experts in education generally omit specific references to a teacher's subject matter knowledge even though their research attests to its importance in defining teaching as work. Compared to societal and school administrative pressures on reading and math teachers, music teachers find themselves to be independent of nearly all bureaucratic control in regard to *what* they teach.

As long as their students perform well in comparison to students in other schools, school administrators tend not to question the music teachers' work, and it is left to the music teachers themselves to examine not only the *what,* but also the *why* and the *how* of their work. Such examination is a professional duty and requires music teachers' willingness to ask questions and find answers about the place of the study of music as artistry as opposed to engaging in music as a social behavior alone.

Questions for Class Discussion

1. In comparing schools in your community, how different do they seem to be from each other in administrative style and sense of school community? What factors do you believe contribute to those differences?

2. If you already are a teacher, how do you see your own role as a staff member in light of the ideas outlined in this chapter? What position do you hold toward your place in the institutional hierarchy? How comfortable are you with it, and how do you negotiate conflicts that arise from being a part of such a hierarchical system?

3. If you are a student preparing to become a teacher, what experiences have you had during your teacher education program that you believe gave you an insight into differences between a professional school music teacher and a professional performer?

3

Music Learning and Teaching as Socially Situated Acts

If you teach someone to cook, make sure there's someone who will eat.

Introduction

It has become commonplace in music education to refer to the learning and teaching of music as identical twins, nearly indistinguishable from each other. This might be true when a 14-year-old spends her spare time teaching herself the electric bass. It may also be the case when a select junior high school group performs to the director's full expectations. But even in the latter of the two scenarios, we cannot assert that teaching and learning came fully together because we do not know, for example, whether all choir members learned as the result of the teacher's instructions: Did they fully understand what they were doing, or did they simply imitate the "leaders" around them? Did they already know the piece from church or camp?

Indeed, music learning happens in many more situations than those encountered during formal instruction in classroom settings or when practicing one's instrument. It can occur by informally watching TV or by listening to one's favorite DVDs or radio stations, by a heated debate with a friend about the latest MTV artists, by attending church choir practice, going to a bar or pub, or simply walking down the street and taking in the sounds. What we remember of those situations is the result of how we connected to the events emotionally and why we have become involved with them in the first place.

Just as there are many varied learning contexts, teaching contexts differ as well. Next to the socialization processes that shape who each teacher is, elementary schools have job realities and requirements different from those of secondary schools. Urban communities confront realities that rural schools do not. Inner-city schools encounter challenges unfamiliar to suburban school environments. Large schools offer greater curricular diversity than do small ones, and teachers in rural settings know firsthand of issues unknown to either suburban or inner-city teaching personnel. A teacher with a long history and tradition in the same school can accomplish things a new teacher cannot.

That many different contextual constellations determine what type of learning and what kind of teaching occur at any given time can be a valuable source of information for music teachers when they plan the *what* and *how* of teaching. At stake is to bring learning and teaching contexts as closely together as possible, a principle of knowledge not unique to us as music educators.

The need to consider contextual constellations when it comes to the transmission of cultural and musical values was first brought to our attention by anthropologists and ethnomusicologists. When they studied musics and cultures other than those dominant in the Western Hemisphere, they found that certain songs and music rituals were performed only during the actual event for which they were intended. Wedding songs could be sung only when a wedding took place; asking tribal members to dance a rite of initiation just for displaying it for onlookers was considered sacrilegious. Music was not rehearsed; instead, it was experienced in the moment for which it was intended. The act of music making and its function in the lives of the people were identical. One generation learned from the other while engaging in the act of doing. Situation and purpose were one. The contextual meaning of the event was the same for all participants, whether they were performers, celebrants, or listeners.

Christopher Small, whose work I describe in greater detail in Chapter 5, has coined the word **musicking (D)** for such a process of being actively and purposefully engaged in a music-making situation. Situated in the "doing" of music, performers and listeners alike share the same experience in different but equally important roles. It often is the essence of what is called community music.

The anthropological and ethnomusicological description of musicking in other cultures does have a bearing not only on the nature of community and ethnic music making but also on how one views what is going on in the music classroom. This is so because, unlike some other school subjects, music is already firmly situated in everybody's life long before school begins. Even young students come with a clear notion of their own music, their favorite songs, TV commercials, or cartoons. They know what music is—at least as it is present in their own heads.

Take, for instance, the answer of a second grader who, when asked what she was doing in music class, responded, "We are not doing music, we are doing *ta ti-ti's.*" Obviously taught by a highly committed Kodály teacher, the child had not (yet) made the connection between what was situated as music in her own head and what happened in class.

Another situation is that of an eighth-grade girls choir working on a Palestrina motet in Latin, a prescribed contest piece. As long as the choir performs the notes in solfège, everybody concentrates on hitting the correct notes and fully complies with the teacher's request to phrase each line as if it were a sentence. Then, ready to add the words, the teacher gives them the translation. One student reacts to the translation by saying out loud, "This is church music. It does not belong here." While some of the girls giggle, others begin to talk among themselves. The rehearsal flow is broken until the teacher seizes the moment and explains to the students the significance of Palestrina in the history of classical vocal music. She clearly makes the best of the situation, but the translation of the Latin text has placed the music in a context with which at least one student was uncomfortable. The music (church) and the context within which it occurred (school) did not properly correspond. Two different sociomusical contexts were perceived to be in conflict with each other, a perception that then resulted in what might be interpreted as disruptive actions by the student.

Earlier in the book I mentioned the middle-school boy enrolled in general music class who asked the teacher why they couldn't ever sing *good* songs in class. That question, too, sent a signal of disconnect between his world of music and what occurred in music class. To address such a disconnect, the teacher might want to give the students the opportunity to debate what, in the students' minds, constitute *good songs*. It is a topic with, first of all, possibly constructive consequences for discussing the significance of musical preferences and styles and their connection to personal as well as group identities as expressed through clothing and language. Secondly, such discussions can lead to productive decisions about future repertoire choice.

This chapter suggests that, as contextually situated behaviors, music learning and teaching processes in the classroom are seldom fully in sync with each other. Effective teachers, however, rely on contextual knowledge to determine "where the students are," a necessary step in taking them "where the teacher wants them to be." This goal should be first among the many that music teachers set for themselves and their classes.

General music specialists frequently express that they strive for their students to have a lifelong love for music. Given that most students have a preconceived idea of their favorite music even before they enter a music classroom, instructional goals must be specific about what styles of music teachers want their students to love or at least learn about. Assuming that classical music is among those styles, one also must ask how broad and comprehensive a teacher's own spectrum of musical awareness is, a question that actually may have as many answers as there are music teachers.

Small Group Discussion 3.1

Share with each other examples in your own life where

- you were your own teacher and learned what you wanted to learn.
- you became aware of the importance of shared contextual knowledge.
- you experienced "out-of-place" music.

How might such examples guide a music teacher in the planning of elective general music courses and/or so-called Introduction to Music classes for nonmusic majors?

Music as a School Subject

Classically trained professional musicians, including most music teachers, believe that music education should focus on (1) preparing young musicians for making music for the rest of their lives; (2) emphasizing the musical repertoire from the classic European tradition whose quality has been time proven; and (3) creating audiences interested in the continuation of that music tradition as well as traditions from other cultures. The objectives focus on the procreation of art for its own sake and on using music and the arts for improving the citizenry's quality of life.

As valuable and as time honored as these objectives are, dealing with quality of life issues is difficult under the best of circumstances. For example, does the appreciation of the so-called finer things in life add to a person's quality of life? Is a life better when we learn to understand the complexities that produce what experts call "good" art? Do we perhaps even imply that those of us who cherish "good art" are therefore better human beings?

These questions aim directly at the purpose of school music: Is its purpose to socialize as many students as possible to the norms and values of classically trained musicians? And should the objectives for music as a required subject differ from the objectives for music as an elective in high school? Finally, to what extent do either of those objectives support general educational objectives that govern an entire school curriculum?

These questions have been answered in different and at times contradicting ways by sociologists, cultural theorists, educationists, and music educators alike. Some of their answers are addressed in greater detail in Chapters 4 and 5. This chapter is based on the premise that music *is* part of the curriculum and that music teachers face different social realities when they work with the musical worlds of their students and their own musical world. It is part of a music teacher's job requirements to work productively with both realities.

When students and teachers share similar musical values and contextual knowledge, chances are good that the students learn and retain what they are supposed to learn. They understand the instructional context and follow the teacher's way of thinking. Barring boredom, the likely result is a positive learning experience for those students.

Dissimilar context knowledge and divergent musical values between students and their teachers can create negative learning experiences if the teacher does not recognize and work with such dissimilarities. For example, it *is* appropriate to provide opportunities for Mariachi bands in schools that have a large Hispanic student population. It makes pedagogical and musical sense to introduce steel drum ensembles in schools located in communities with predominantly Cuban immigrants and fiddling to students with an Irish background. Also, the teaching of guitar and accordion, popular in many Eastern European countries, may open musical doors that otherwise may stay closed to many an immigrant student from that part of the world.

Any efforts to connect music learning familiar to students outside of school with formal learning in school can strengthen a student's social as well as musical self and a school community's identity and pride. Music teachers can be important contributors in both regards and open the doors to new avenues of learning in general, not only musical learning.

Interview Project 3.1

Ask two to three younger boys and girls in your family or neighborhood the types of music they like and listen to in their spare time. Compare this to what you remember of yourself when you were their age.

Music Listening in the Classroom

The overriding purpose of music instruction in public schools today lies in encouraging students to perform, listen, and respond to music knowingly and with discrimination. This means that, next to playing an instrument of their choice, students are expected to learn to articulate what it is they hear in the performed music, contrast what they hear to other pieces they have performed or listened to, and make informed judgments about similarities and differences between the pieces. Developing such skills in the students takes time. Therefore teachers tend to shy away from spending class time on listening tasks when they need more rehearsal time.

Substituting actual listening time with rehearsing is an understandable decision but sociologically perhaps not necessarily a wise one. Not wanting to spend instructional time on talking is also reasonable because it is much condoned by conductors and pedagogues alike. Furthermore, the teaching of listening skills is difficult because how each of us listens in the privacy of our own homes differs so substantially from the listening environments schools offer.

Outside of school, even listening to music while driving one's car or while simultaneously engaging in other nonmusical tasks are, in the ears of most individuals, students included, not any less important activities than listening to music in a music appreciation class. Teachers and, especially, well-trained professional performers of mostly classical music tend to be uncomfortable with the notion that listening to music for purposes of relaxation in the privacy of one's home may be as valuable as listening to a Bach fugue during a music appreciation class or, better yet, performing it. From a sociological perspective, all of these activities are of equal value, albeit for different reasons, because each activity is socially important to the people who are engaged in it. The activity defines the setting and vice versa. From a pedagogical perspective, of course, guided listening tasks are a must in the classroom setting.

Awareness of the difference between music listening outside of school musical situations and those created in rehearsal and classroom settings is especially relevant to teaching general music classes, music appreciation courses, or even introductory courses to popular music. If, in the latter, we have the students listen in class to a rock band or rap artist, it occurs "out of context." Similarly, listening to country and western music in the commonly quiet and somewhat academic environment of a college music class might feel awkward even to someone who thoroughly enjoys dancing a two-step in a honky-tonk with a live-music band.

These are the reasons why the teacher should be up front with the students about the fact that music listening in and outside of school differ and that one should not be confused with the other. Once it has become clear to the students that the purpose of listening in school lies in making comparisons between music of different styles and times, students are often quite willing to listen to music styles that most directly precede their own immediate musical culture, such as the music of their parents or grandparents. Today, this would touch on such old classics as, for example, the Beatles, Elvis Presley, the Rolling Stones, Sting, Led Zeppelin, or other early rock musicians. The teacher can then trace further back into the history of music, from folk jazz to early jazz to early 20th-century European music, as far back as the school calendar allows. At all times, though, the music should be brought back and compared to the music of today (whatever "today" means to any generation).

When talking to students, one often finds that outside the realm of traditional music schools, the term *classical* is relative. For example, some film music selections taken from Barber, Prokofiev, Beethoven, or Saint-Saens have become popular, that is, favorites, among people who might otherwise categorically state that classical music is not for them.

The term *classical,* also, is ambiguous. Young people call today's music *contemporary* while classical musicians tend to subsume all of that music as *pop,* a term that does not do justice to the many categories by which the music industry describes today's musics.

The confusion in music terminology poses just the first among several challenges for someone who seeks to develop engaging listening lesson models and programs for students of different ages. A second challenge lies in staying abreast of the constantly changing music scene, both in the realm of music as art form and music as a socially engaged *doing* by younger generations. Third, listening tasks should always be combined with performance, a recommendation that also suggests the use of available computer technology and software packages, such as Apple's iLife *Garage Band*[1] to engage the students in *active* music making, listening, and arranging.

Interview Project 3.2

Interview music directors who work in different cultural settings (e.g., church, community groups, after-school youth programs, public and private schools) about the way they select music activities and repertoire.

---

[1] http://www.osviews.com/modules.php?op=modload&name=News&file=article&sid=719

Music Teachers as Bridge Builders
Between Different Communities

In the eyes of most students, their parents, the school administrators, and the school community at large, the musical and pedagogical choices teachers make are seen as reflections of the teacher's own personal values. Factually, of course, instructional decisions are often based less on a teacher's personal preference than on budgetary reasons, prescribed objectives (either by the state or locally), and by programmatic concerns, such as seasonal concerts and expected or required participation in music competitions and festivals. Nonetheless and unless told otherwise, students equate what goes on in music classes or rehearsals with their music teacher's own musical values. Musical selections, rehearsed and performed in concert, symbolize in the eyes and ears of the student performers and the school community alike what the teacher stands for musically and culturally.

Teachers who are aware of this fact work with such knowledge in several ways. One, they send the message that they have open musical minds and they value the opinions and taste of their students, parents, and nonmusic colleagues. They do so by letting the students have a say in selecting music of a stylistically wide array of technically comparable choices. Or a choral director places similarity of texts into the center of a concert, keeping a recurrent theme throughout a stylistically diverse collection of songs.

Two, the teacher can engage the students in a project in which they find out from parents, friends, and neighbors what type of music they might like to hear in the next year's winter and/or spring concert. This requires a prepared list from which the school community is asked to select a specified number.

Three, the teacher could program compositions whose composers are connected either by nationality, stylistic contrasts, or significance in the context of important events that have shaped the country's or state's history. Such programming would allow for the inclusion of multicultural and ethnic music, a dimension of music making that, if commensurate with general school policies, would require smaller ensembles and performance practices than what has become so common in most American high schools.

Ultimately, understanding the significance of letting one's programming reflect a wide range of repertoire that is meaningful to the student performers and their parents can go a long way in strengthening the school community through music. Not everyone subscribes to this objective, but, given the position music teachers have in the school community, being considered a positive force in the community is an important role. The music teacher, through the music curriculum itself, becomes a bridge builder between the worlds of school communities, music communities, and political communities by taking into consideration not only the prevailing values of the student body and local school community but also the values espoused by other constituent groups who make decisions about the purpose of education in society and the place of the arts in it.

School Communities and Music Communities:
Three Sociological Perspectives

Communities, be they formed by shared geographical terrain, political bound-aries, or special interests such as music or education, are imbedded in the conven-tions and confronted by similar issues with which society at large is faced: population stratification, equality of educational opportunities for children of all social classes as well as types of upbringing, and concerns of equal opportunities for all races, classes, and genders. Sociologists can help music teachers to under-stand to what extent each individual either shapes or is shaped by those commu-nal forces, and how such forces relate to each other in the entirety of society.

To state it broadly, sociological thinking helps us observe and explain how hu-mans organize specific knowledge and experiences while living with each other in groups that differ in beliefs, classes, gender, age, and economic status. As teachers we become informed about why and how humans interact with each other for spe-cific purposes across different social, demographic, as well as economic contexts and as communities of different racial and ethnic identities. Those identities bring with them varying views toward the reasons for education and formal learning, as well as the place of music, culture, and religion in those reasons.

More than 30 years ago, Straus and Nelson (1968) stated it quite simply: "Con-temporary sociologists are interested in explanations of the way societies and so-cial groups behave" (p. 1). Those behaviors are always connected to tangible purposes that mandate the interactions. Thus, to study the behavior of individuals in smaller or larger group settings, the purposes for which and contexts in which the behaviors take place must be integral to all sociological examinations. Musi-cal behaviors provide one such context; others might be behaviors during political rallies, religious or family gatherings, athletic events, professional meetings, or leisure-time pursuits.

Within the many different contexts and varying purposes that provide the basis for human interactions, sociologists examine a host of questions, many of which are interrelated. For example, one might ask how specific societal groups interact-ing with music, sports, or politics are stratified according to gender, race, socio-economic background, and ethnicity. One might seek to identify and compare the norms and values that either unite or set groups of individuals apart from each other. Or, regardless of shared purposes within a group, one can (1) examine the hierarchical relationships among all of the individuals in a group, (2) determine the degree of normative similarities and differences between them, and/or (3) as-certain the extent to which feelings of alienation between individuals hinder or propel successful musical, political, or religious interactions.

Sociologists study such issues from three particular perspectives that are help-ful in understanding the field of sociology in general and can also become relevant to understanding the field of music education from a sociological viewpoint. Most readily identifiable are the so-called macro and micro views (see, for example, Hechter & Horne, 2003; Huber, 1991; Lipset & Hofstadter, 1968; Tepperman &

Rosenberg, 1998). In between these two positions lies the interactive perspective, also called *interactionism,* a term with varying meanings in different disciplines. In the remainder of this chapter I use the term as it has been described by Bulmer (1977), Collins (1994, 2004), and Blumer (2004).

Figure 3.1 visualizes the three sociological perspectives in their relationship to each other. The macro view might be described as a bird's-eye view of society as a political cultural, religious, educational, and/or social system. The micro view takes a bottoms-up view of such a system, and "bringing both views together" is the interactionist perspective. Depending on the purpose for which one looks at society and its groups as a system, different sociological theories have emerged that seek to explain why and how individuals in society cope and interact with

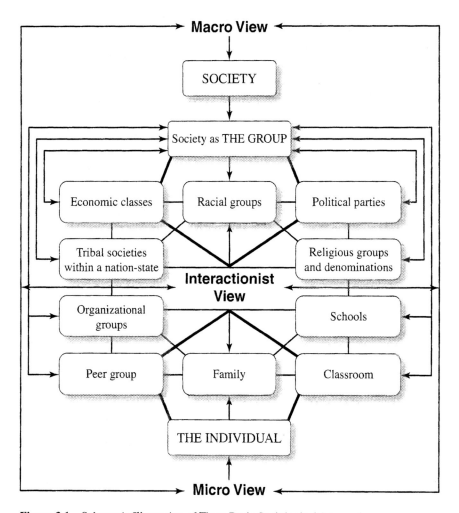

Figure 3.1 Schematic Illustration of Three Basic Sociological Approaches

each other in the context of political, religious, cultural, educational, and social challenges.

Macro sociologists look at society and the groups in it as a whole, comparing their own society to how other societies cope. Such comparisons are based on large-scale examinations. The micro view takes behaviors of specific individuals as the springboard for articulating reasons that might explain the behaviors of an entire group in terms of the specific challenges observed individuals face. Whether a group is a person's family, his or her peers, a religious congregation, or a school community, we assume the individual's choices and behaviors are not so much the result of his or her own choices but deeply rooted in the norms and values of the group of which the individual is or wants to be a part. Applied to education, the group one might study could be the particular school a pupil attends, a classroom, the entire teaching staff, or all fourth-grade teachers in a school or school district.

The interactionist view acknowledges society "as a loose network of related parts in a constant flux" (Meighan & Siraj-Blatchford, 2003, p. 14). Interactionists "tend to look two ways, both at the patterns of society stressed by the macro sociologists and at the work and negotiations that individuals accomplish in keeping society going, as stressed in the micro perspectives" (Meighan & Blatchford, 2003, p. 14). Sometimes also touted as a micro perspective, interactionist research methodology differs from that of micro sociology in the role the researcher plays in the investigative process itself. Most importantly, the researcher is integral to that which is being investigated. As each social setting is explained contextually, the researcher's own role in the setting under investigation is part of that context. However, not even the smallest social unit of inquiry, such as one single classroom, is independent of the larger contexts that frame the inquiry. The researcher's own role therefore is one such context; the school and its location another; the teacher's and the students' social-economic, cultural, and musical backgrounds and biographies a third sphere of context. All of the contextual spheres *inter-react* with each other at any given moment during which we are engaged with each other in the research process. Each and any of these contexts, therefore, are influenced by the racial, economic, cultural, and political constellations that shape the life of each person, including that of the researcher.

Unlike interactionists, social psychologists tend to analyze dyadic relationships by either analyzing interactions between two or more individuals or how and why individuals relate to a particular issue or subject matter the way they do. For example, an individual's musical taste and dress choices can be interpreted as a matter of personal choice or background but also as the result of certain power constellations among peer groups and cliques. Both social psychologists and social interactionists acknowledge these possibilities; however, interactionists look at dress codes and musical preferences as indicators of social belonging, affiliation, and self-identification throughout a person's life, not simply during one's adolescent years. As such, dress codes and musical preferences become subjects of sociological analysis. In that instance, musical taste or choices of what to wear cease to be personal choices. Musical predilections, for example, become symbols of group norms and values throughout one's life. Sociologically, they serve as indicators of how individuals view themselves in the hierarchy of subgroups of which they are or want to be a part.

The type of research that interactionists engage in requires them not to disturb the social setting in which the research takes place. The method, shared with many social psychologists of today, is called *participant observation*. It is a technique in which the researcher (1) seeks to become a member of the group(s) of individuals he or she wishes to learn about; (2) spends time getting to know the person(s) in those groups; and (3) abstains from research jargon, experimentation, and intimidating research apparatuses and designs. Any such project also tends to take place over a long period of time, a process referred to as *longitudinal research*.

In contrast, micro- and macrosociological analyses generally rely on nonparticipant observational methods. In this process, one employs large-scale surveys and questionnaires and analyzes the resulting data through statistical methods. Although such tools allow one to collect a larger data pool than is possible with individual interviews, the drawbacks are that those being interviewed might not feel at ease with answering personal questions or be truthful about their relationship to other group members.

Macro, Micro, and Interactive Analyses in Their Application to Music and Music Education

Figure 3.2 is a conceptual adaptation of Figure 3.1 to situations in which sociological analyses may be applied to music and music education. More subgroups and cultures than those listed in Figure 3.2 are possible. What is shown serves merely as an example for possible purposes for which one might want to study the relationship of society and music/culture from the macro-, micro-, or interactive sociological perspective.

Macrosociology, Music, and Music Education

When music scholars look at music from a macro perspective, they study the cultural, ethical, and musical norms and values of different ethnic groups or socioeconomic classes in society. Such analyses are usually theoretical because they are broad based. They might address musical taste as a construct across socioeconomic and geographical boundaries and compare music instructional processes across countries and cultures. In fact, early sociologists as well as music sociologists generally took a macro view of music in society, often describing that relationship in global terms and across cultures.

Today's music educators interested in a macro view of the field might (1) examine the political ideology behind the educational system itself that gives music the position in the curriculum that it has; (2) determine the impact of the mass

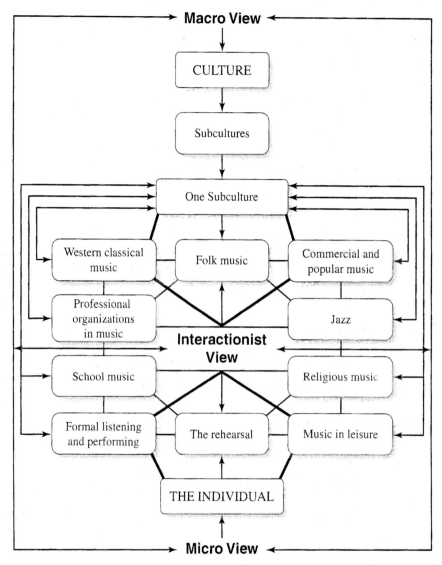

Figure 3.2   Sociological Approaches Applied to the Study of Music Learning and Teaching

media and the music industry on music education practices in schools; and (3) study the relationship of cultural policies on school music and music teacher training. Such questions would also include whether an educational system is centralized or decentralized and how such a configuration affects the music curricula nation- and statewide as well as locally.

Macro analyses in music education might also focus on schools as socialization forces as a whole, placing what music teachers do within the larger function of schooling as a sociopolitical mandate. Teachers and students are thus seen as functioning parts of a larger machine: an intricate system of schools, school districts, and state- as well as nationwide educational and cultural policies.

Microsociology, Music, and Music Education

Tia DeNora's (2000) *Music in Everyday Life* is an example of microanalyzing how nonprofessionals describe their relationship to specific music in particular social situations. The author retained her role as an outsider to the group of adult women she interviewed in various metropolitan areas and small towns in the United Kingdom and the United States.

Microanalyses applied to the nature of school music might involve a comparison of music teachers as a group to science and math teachers, focusing on the importance of subject matter as defining how each of the groups function within a school system. One might ask, for example, how music teachers differ from or are similar to math teachers, language arts teachers, or visual arts teachers. Do they think of themselves as artists first and pedagogues second? Do they continue to grow as musicians while they teach? Do they grow as pedagogues? If so, how, and in what direction? Or one might want to do what White (1964) did: observe and analyze differences among music teachers themselves—band directors, choir directors, and string specialists compared to general music teachers at the elementary and secondary level of instruction.

Interactionism, Music, and Music Education

Projects emanating from interactionist interests are best conducted if the teachers themselves find out what their students think (see, among others, Adler, 2002; Roberts, 1994). If one wanted to investigate how members in a music ensemble interacted with each other and the director, the teacher himself or herself actually could (1) make those observations over a long period of time, (2) take ongoing field notes in an unobtrusive manner, and (3) interpret the students' behaviors and responses in a contextually familiar environment.

Extant studies in music education that have employed interactionist research questions and methods are rare. Although a number of investigations including numerous dissertations have used what is known as qualitative designs, the researchers usually were nonparticipant observers and sought ways to be as unobtrusive in the classroom as possible. The studies also lacked a longitudinal time span.

In conclusion, to fully understand music teaching and learning as two distinctly different social components in the field of education, all three perspectives, the macro, micro, and interactive, are needed if we want to know how music, society, and schools relate to each other in the broadest political sense and in the most personal context of one classroom in one school. No one perspective can capture the complexities involved in such relationships, a fact the remaining chapters of this book underscore.

As music teachers begin to look for the sociomusical givens that determine their daily work, they may begin to see patterns of behaviors that, once understood as integral to how different social groups work, cease to be threatening or frustrating. Knowing why people act the way they do helps in responding in an informed way. Power structures become transparent and different social contexts of learning and teaching can be accepted as realities typical of what defines a music teacher's job. We become aware of what it takes to understand the needs of the different groups of people with whom we communicate directly and indirectly every day. Such awareness may truly lead to empowerment.

Questions for Class Discussion

1.   Together brainstorm how you could engage in some observation projects where you, as the member of a group of your choice, can make long-term observations and converse with other members of the group in such a way that you get the information you are looking for. Identify the main questions that emerge during the process of planning such a project.

2.   How do you react to different types of music present in today's culture with which you are not very familiar? How would you educate yourself about such music in a way that would allow you to incorporate it in your teaching?

3.   Considering the different styles of music that exist side-by-side in our society, take the position of a macro-sociologist, a micro-sociologist, and an interactionist, respectively, and discuss how they might suggest we teach about music as a social phenomenon. Include in your discussion how each of the three perspectives might impact research on the diversity of musical styles in our society.

4

Music and Social Context

Macro, Micro, and Interactive Perspectives in Selected Texts on the Sociology of Music

Build new beliefs that reframe, refine, and, when necessary,
replace old beliefs. And then . . . continue the cycle.

Introduction

In this chapter, I describe books that are (1) either titled or subtitled "A Sociology of Music," (2) have become readily available in the English language, and (3) can be categorized as macro, micro, and interactive approaches toward understanding music as a social rather than purely aesthetic phenomenon. At the forefront of topics addressed in these books are (1) the interactions that take place between performers and their audiences in particular performance settings, and (2) the role of music for its own sake as compared to its social purposes, that is, its use during recreational or ceremonial functions. Those functions are shown to relate directly to the image professional performers have of themselves as entertainer and/or artist, an issue that impacts on their occupational identity as well.

A perusal of the books, makes it clear that most writers have focused on the macro perspective of sociology by suggesting particular theories about (1) the power of sociopolitical and economic forces on musics of all types and in all cultures, and (2) the place of particular communities in the music-making traditions of a particular geographical location. In doing so, the authors drew some historical comparisons between music in different societies and discussed the coexistence of musical subcultures in a society.

Furthermore, the referenced works do not always agree on the relationship between musical and social meanings in a work or in the act of music making. One scholar clearly separates the two meanings; another might argue their interconnectedness. A third scholar determines the relative value of a piece of music almost exclusively by the purpose (musical or social) for which it was composed, and a fourth writer might rely on how performing musicians themselves describe the meaning they derive from making music in specific contexts and for socially situated purposes.

Perusing extant works on the sociology of music therefore makes it clear that the question of musical versus social meaning is central to thinking about music in sociological terms. This chapter invites you to join in the debate of how social interactions between individuals and groups for the purpose of listening to and making music can lead to discoveries about who we are as social and musical beings.

Weber and Adorno: Two Important Names Beyond Music

Max Weber (1864–1920) and Theodor W. Adorno (1903–1969), historically not only two of the most influential thinkers in the sociology of music but also in general sociology, political theory, and economic theory, are considered macro-sociologists. Weber (1921/1958) contributed significantly to music scholarship in his landmark essay *The Rational and Social Foundations of Music*. Adorno's introductory text to a sociology of music, first published in Germany in 1962, was one of the first to actually present what a sociology of music might entail.

Weber's *The Rational and Social Foundations of Music*

The 1958 translation of Weber's technical and dense German text (originally published in 1921) was subtitled by its translators a "Sociology of Music." The translators, too, organized the essay into chapters and gave it an introduction that considerably eases comprehending Weber's original writing. One of the translators, Johannes Riedel, has a visible connection to music education in the United States through his very readable article "The Function of Sociability in the Sociology of Music and Music Education," published in the *Journal of Research for Music Education* (Riedel, 1964).

Weber's "Theory of Rationalization"

One cannot understand Weber's treatise on music without some knowledge of his 1905 book *The Protestant Ethic and the Spirit of Capitalism* (1905/1920/2002). In it he sets out to prove that the Protestant ethic is at the root of Western economic theory. The latter is characterized by a drive for rational efficiency and economic profit, both of which together drive Western societies' quest for material wealth and scientific discoveries.

Rational efficiency is the result of a process Weber calls rationalization, one of the most general elements in Weber's theory. The process of rationalization is responsible for an increased division of labor, bureaucracy, and mechanization of all aspects of modern Western societies. The result, in Weber's view, has been "depersonalization, oppressive routine, rising secularism"[1] and an increased loss of individual freedom (see also Gerth & Mills, 1946).

To test the validity of his general economic theory, Weber needed proof for the validity of his construct of rationalization. Therefore, as an economist he applied his studies to many different disciplines, among them the arts, religion, and, especially, music.

Weber looked for rationality in music by theorizing about (1) the relationship of harmony to melody; (2) prediatonic scales in relationship to Western scale systems; (3) the impact of the rationalization of scale systems on the role of the musician as magician, virtuoso, and professional; (4) polyvocality and polysonority in relation to music rationalization; and, finally, (5) instruments and the rationalization of nonharmonic tones through equalization and tempering.

Entirely focused on the acoustic properties of Western music, Weber used his knowledge of physics and tonal relationships to show why Western classical sounds, allowing for establishing harmonic relationships between pitches, should be considered superior to non-Western pitch systems. The superiority, he maintained, was not related to aesthetic qualities inherent in a given musical piece but to the process of rationalization inherent in the Pythagorean theory of sound. He claimed it to be the most efficient tonal system of sound among all other systems.

Adorno's *Introduction to the Sociology of Music*

As a founding member of the so-called Frankfurt school of critical theory, established by Max Horkheimer (1895–1973) during his exile in the United States, Adorno fully developed critical theory as a post–World War II offshoot of Marxism as a social philosophy. A composer himself, Adorno was especially interested in examining the place and function of music in society from a neo-Marxist perspective.

Karl Marx (1818–1883) had sought to explain how modern societies (from feudalism to late capitalism) have evolved historically and materially. He thus had interpreted all human activities and artifacts as reflections of the societal conditions of their time. The latter are shaped by those who own the means of production (those who "hold the purse string," i.e., the haves) as they control those who work for them (the have-nots).

Whenever one group exercises control over another, an element of alienation enters into the relationship. The degree of alienation is a vehicle for identifying power relationships, a key concept in critical theory and one of the major theoretical macrosociological positions today.

Like Marxist theory, the method of reasoning in critical theory lies in the use of what is called dialectic reasoning, a method of argumentation that historically is rooted in German philosophical scholarship, namely that of G. W. F.

[1] Elwell, Frank (1996). *The Sociology of Max Weber*. Retrieved July 28, 2004, from http://www.faculty.rsu.edu/~felwell/Theorists/Weber/Whome.htm

Hegel (1770–1831). It involves both a thesis (a statement of what is) and its antithesis (a statement posing as the opposite of the thesis). This juxtaposition leads to a dynamic tension in the argument itself that never gets resolved, only propelled forward by means of a synthesis that, in turn, becomes the next thesis. The process is open ended and without a preestablished conclusion. Truth lies in the process of developing the argument itself, not, as is the case in propositional logic, in its conclusion.

The application of dialectic reasoning to social issues in society is called critical theory because, following Marxism, it asks about the economic and political constellations that cause human behavior to be what it is. Adorno used dialectic logic in his examination of the methods by which empirical realities can and should be researched. This examination included the study of music and music behavior.

Small Group Discussion 4.1

Find examples of dialectic logic and living in your everyday life.

Adorno's Application of Critical Theory to Music

Throughout his career, Adorno wrote about "the changing role of (art) music in contemporary mass society, as compared with the past" (Etzkorn, 1973, p. 19). He contrasted art music and its origin to how popular music is created through the mass media and technology, consisting at the time the book was written mainly of radio and television.

Adorno's analyses of radio and television music focused on the "disconnect" between what he believed to be an individual's real musical needs and media-created musical needs for "the masses." Individuals as members of large groups become prey to the free market system and are controlled by laws of supply and demand ("laws of the marketplace") rather than by their own free will.

In Adorno's view, collective musical needs created by the media are artificial because they do not correspond to the actual musical values an individual holds. He called this phenomenon the social alienation of music, a characteristic he saw present in all media-created music.

Adorno argued that what classical music lovers call serious or art music is characterized by a somewhat greater autonomy from commercial pressures and manipulations than is mass-produced popular music. Thus, although he saw some need for sociological analyses of art music, he did not engage in it. He did acknowledge, however, that classical music can also become socially alienated music, when, for instance, it is used in shopping malls, hotels, or elevators as background music. In other words, whenever music is used for commercial rather than aesthetic purposes, it ceases to be art music because it loses its authentic purpose of art for art's sake. He called this type of music "consumer music."

Next to his philosophical position on the nature of popular and classic music and their historical and economical positions in society, the *Introduction to a Sociology of Music* contains a hierarchically tiered typology of listeners, musical styles, and genres. It is based on Adorno's analytical insights into the compositional complexity of different musical works as it correlates to listeners' degrees of musically informed responses. The more complex a composition and the more a listener hears that complexity, the more authentic the listening experience. Popular music, in Adorno's view, can not lead to an authentic listening experience because the music is manipulated for purposes of market control.

Adorno's position on popular and classical music as being either fully market controlled or free of those pressures was adopted by a number of music scholars. It also led to the rather widespread, but recently contested, view that sociology is for the study of popular music what musicology is for the study of art music.

Today, critical theorists interested in the study of music hold that good works of music exist in all categories of musical style, from jazz to rock to reggae to salsa. What labels a piece as good lies in the way it is produced, composed, and brought to the audience's attention. Again, the criterion remains that of authenticity of purpose.

For example, if the recording artist has an active part in the artistic/creative process, the music is authentic and therefore valuable. Once principles of market research and consumer behavior govern the production of a piece of music for the purpose of mass distribution, then the music must be considered alienated from the artistic process. The music is nonauthentic and, thus, of little worth and value.

Small Group Discussion 4.2

Discuss what high school students of today might call "authentic music." What is authentic music in your own experience? How useful is the term in your view to determine what to include in music listening lessons for a general music classroom in junior high school classes of a large inner-city school located nearest to where you attend college?

Other Texts on a Sociology of Music

Whereas Weber and Adorno had definite theoretical positions that held their respective sociologies of music together, other texts did not. Perhaps that is also one reason why, compared to the attention Weber and Adorno received from their publications, subsequent writers have had far less impact in the Americas.

Silbermann's *Sociology of Music*

Alphons Silbermann (1957/1963) was a macrosociologist who spoke about music as a social science, analyzing how musical experiences are socially determined. He clearly viewed the structure of sociomusical groups (e.g., professional orchestras, community music groups, etc.) as functionally embedded in the cultural fabric of society. To make this point, he outlined group- and function-specific behaviors for those groups and showed the consequences of such knowledge for proactively planning and structuring activities for musicians, nonmusicians, and audiences.

Unlike many macrosociologists who addressed the place of music as a social phenomenon, Silbermann insisted on being true to empiricism by arguing that a sociology of music needed factual observations about how music functions in society prior to interpreting the meaning people attach to such functions. He thus argued for an inductive approach toward research, a process by which observations about behaviors precede the development of explanations why those behaviors occur. Because of his belief in the importance of data preceding a theory, he continued to collect observations (data) without ever actually developing a philosophical position by which to explain those observations.

Supičić's *Music in Society: A Guide to the Sociology of Music*

Ivo Supičić (pronounced soo-*pee*-tsh-itsh) first published his book in 1964 in Serbo-Croatian, a language spoken in the country then known as Yugoslavia. The book focused on two purposes. First, "the subject and methods of the sociology of music, its position and boundaries in respect to musicology, and most especially, its relationship to the aesthetics of music and to music history" needed to be determined (1987, p. xi). Secondly, Supičić wished "to ascertain what the sociology of music as a separate scholarly discipline embraces, where its investigation leads, and, finally, what its position is vis-à-vis sociology in general" (p. xi). Both objectives together, "the study *on* the sociology of music as an autonomous and specialized discipline, and that of research *within* the sociology of music itself" were the focus of this formidable book.

True to its objectives, the book is divided into two parts. The first part, titled "The Sociology of Music," entails two chapters, each of which is divided into several sections. Chapter 1, "The Sociology of Music and Related Disciplines," provides an overview of the different approaches toward the sociology of music as they existed during the time the book was first written. It includes scholars from musicology, ethnomusicology, aesthetics, sociology, and philosophy from both Germany and France.

Chapter 2, "Subject and Methods," addresses the sociohistorical and socioartistic conditions music sociologists consider when asking their questions. The chapter also refers to what the French call *milieu,* the context within which observations about human behavior take place. The ramifications, according to

Supičić, are clear in that empirical-experimental methods take variables out of context, in his view a sociologically untenable approach to research. It is a view he shares with critical theorists as well as interactionists in the field of education.

The second part of the book, "Music in Society," has ten chapters, each of which is subdivided into numerous sections. Reflecting Supičić's desire to offer a comprehensive account of what a sociology of music can and should be, the chapters deal with music in its many social manifestations and functions, the latter including the roles and functions of the professional musician in society. Given the detailed examination of the topics, each of which should be of interest to U.S. music educators, the book has received surprisingly little attention.

Kaplan: Toward a Social Theory for the Arts

Max Kaplan (1911–1999) articulated the need for a sociology of music in his *Foundations and Frontiers of Music Education* (1966) as well as in his 1951 dissertation *The Musician in America: A Study of His Social Roles; Introduction to a Sociology of Music.* His interest in bringing music sociological thinking to the attention of music educators originated in his work on music as a vehicle of recreational pursuits (Kaplan, 1952), a topic he eventually expanded to include all of the arts (Kaplan, 1990).

A good social theory about the arts, Kaplan argued, must first of all include both their aesthetic as well as their social functions. Second, the theory should encompass the perspectives of those who create the arts, distribute, and listen or view them. Third, the model must address the role of education in any artistic development. And, fourth, all aspects ought to be connected in the form of a matrix. He presented those four requirements in his 1990 book.

Specific to music education, *Foundations and Frontiers of Music Education* (1966) speaks about the social order and the arts and the social as well as artistic values that determine different types of social order. At play here are the varying social and aesthetic functions that the arts have in the lives of people. From those functions emanate different social roles of musicians, which are perceived in varying ways by nonmusic communities.

Vital to understanding what Kaplan calls the central values in the occupation of musicians are the personality and case studies on musicians in which Kaplan mixes psychological concepts with sociological ones. This mix results in pools of data not always comparable to each other because the questions psychologists and sociologists ask and the ways in which they answer them differ.

From describing the case studies of musicians, Kaplan then speaks to the relationship between audiences and society in general, a topic that eventually leads to concerns about music education and music in the community. Only here does he mention music education as a profession and the consequences for such knowledge for music education research. Specific to the role a music educator holds in society, he depicts the many relationships as shown in Figure 4.1, referring to those roles and relationships as "loyalties and obligations" (p. 69).

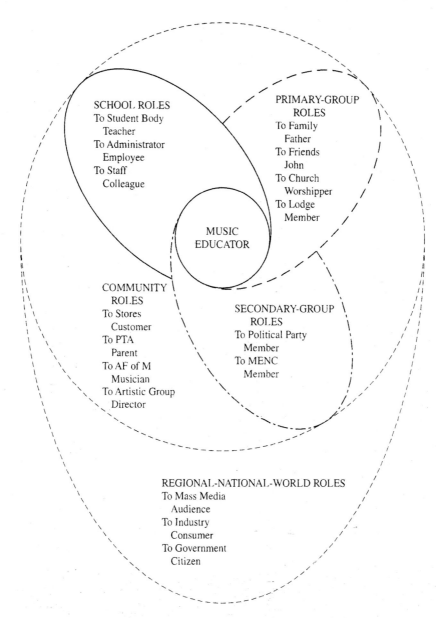

Figure 4.1 Kaplan's Scheme of Social Roles, Loyalties, and Obligations of the Music Educator (1966, p. 69)*

Like Supičić's text, Kaplan makes use of components inherent in macro-, micro-, and interactive analyses. But he also refers to psychological models of research to a greater degree than do other music sociologists. Finally, Kaplan brings home the close relationship between music as recreation and as a school discipline, pointing to the consequences of taking seriously and working with musical values and meaning inherent in both social settings. What is work for one group of people is recreation for another. "School music" *can* be the same as what people listen to outside of school, but it is not always so. Depending on the circumstances, the differences can be great, at other times small; both cases have implications for music education.

Small Group Discussion 4.3

Discuss your view of the relationship between music as leisure pursuit and music as school subject. Identify similarities and differences as you have experienced them.

Etzkorn's *Music & Society. The Later Writings of Paul Honigsheim*

Like Kaplan's book, the Etzkorn/Honigsheim text (1973, 1989) was fully intended as a sociology of music for an English-speaking readership. K. Peter Etzkorn, one of Honigsheim's students, published the book. Etzkorn used his own judgment about what materials, gathered by his teacher, were to be included in the book. But he also lets the reader know which issues Honigsheim himself would have selected, namely, "The Intended Meanings of Music," "The Cultural Evaluation of Music," "The Socioeconomic Position of the Musician," "The Social Structure of the Audience," and "The Social Forms and Musical Forms" (Etzkorn, 1973, p. 32). According to J. Allan Beegle, a colleague of Honigsheim at Michigan State University, one reason why Honigsheim never completed his envisioned sociology of music was his struggle to understand the American popular music culture, a component pivotal to any sociology of music (Etzkorn, 1973, p. ix).

Etzkorn provides a very readable introductory chapter to the book. In it he gives an overview of different music sociological theories in an attempt to systematize the many different sociological schools of thought that have prevailed in Europe since the late 19th century. The 1989 edition further expands the bibliography but keeps almost everything else as it appeared in the first edition.

Of the various theories outlined by Etzkorn, he details several Eastern European approaches toward thinking about music in sociological terms. Such thinking was steeped in theories derived from a philosophy that embraced the political-economic doctrine of what were then the Soviet Union and its satellite countries. Today, one should distinguish Marxism as a philosophy from its economic application in autocratic political systems, a distinction that is at the core of the Frankfurt school of critical theory.

In addition to addressing music sociology and Marxism in some detail, Etzkorn asks the question of how the two disciplines of musicology and sociology have interacted with each other in the early days of music sociological thinking. For many musicologists, sociology has become a tool that simply aids them in the musicological analysis of a composition. The analytical focus lies on the musical work, the product, itself.

Other music scholars, ethnomusicologists in particular, employ musicological analyses to illuminate how individuals interact socially with music at any given time and under specific social conditions. The musicological analysis helps clarify music making as a social act for which the composition is a tool. Etzkorn suggested that both types of scholarship, sociology and musicology, should be considered of equal value because a *musicological sociology* can be as useful as a *sociological musicology*. I share his view because music teachers rely on both types of knowledge to build a solid bridge between the world of music as experts understand it and the way music novices see and hear it.

DaSilva, Blasi, and Dees's *The Sociology of Music*

Combining macro, micro, and interactionist thinking, DaSilva et al. (1984) ground music in a broad-based, interpretive social theory that can be beneficial for curriculum discussions in music education. The theory is interpretive because it follows what philosophers call the hermeneutic method, an approach toward scholarship that combines descriptive and qualitative investigative techniques. It is a useful method for writing critical self-reflections to improve one's teaching strategies.

The first three chapters (music as a mentality, participation in music, and social organization and music) touch on many of the issues covered in other sociology of music books: (1) the social nature of all music making, (2) the relativity of social contexts and musical meaning, (3) the dialectic nature of such realities as well as the diverse roles of musicians and audiences in today's society, and (4) the social inequality of musicians' work. Illustrative and eclectic case studies comprise the fourth chapter, which includes the relationship of costumes to music performance, the various styles in banjo playing as indicators of how musical organizations are structured, social symbolism in Joplin's opera *Tremonisha,* and the social content of Villa-Lobos's *A Prole do Bebê.*

Pointing to the social order of which music is an integral part, DaSilva stresses the relativity of musical realities. The case studies especially speak to the value of interactionist theories that allow one to understand the conduct, that is, the behaviors of people as indicators, or symbols, of social self-image: who one wants to be or how one believes one needs to act under certain circumstances and in different musical contexts.

Much in the book is implied rather than described in detail. Social orders are only referred to in general terms for performers and audiences. Nonetheless, the overall message of the book is important for music educators: Different musical contexts imply different codes of behavior. Most music performers who make a living by playing in different venues know this and act accordingly: A jazz setting requires different behaviors from that evident in a rock concert, a church, or symphony concert. Dress codes, language, and the interactions with the audiences change in each of these settings and become second nature to music professionals.

Martin's Sounds and Society. Themes in the Sociology of Music

A more recent effort to introduce a sociology of music to an English-speaking readership is not a comprehensive textbook. Rather, Peter Martin (1995) describes his book as an attempt to develop an understanding of music from a distinctly sociological perspective. Contrasting his perspective to those that emanate from cultural studies or social psychology, Martin believes that "general sociological discourse can be employed in ways that enhance our understanding of music and of the social contexts in which it is created, performed, and heard" (p. x). Referring to Silbermann, Adorno, and Supičić, Martin (1995) contends that "none of them can stand as authoritative basis for the sociologically informed study of music" (p. vii). This is so, he asserts, because all three scholars focus more on European art music than on music performed and found all over the world.

Marxism and Critical Theory as Analytical Centerpieces

After introducing the reader to the relationship between sociology and music, Martin then adopts Marxism and critical theory as two of the most important theoretical stances in sociological thinking today. Both theories support the notion that individuals construct meaning as the result of where they are situated socially and culturally. Applied to music, musical meaning is not inherent in the music itself but is constructed as the result of our own experiences with it.

Martin embraces this viewpoint and shows how the social construction of musical meaning impacts as well as is impacted by the language of music, forms of music, socialization experiences, and commonsense knowledge. Especially Martin's focus on language acquisition adds a dimension to thinking about music learning from a sociological perspective that, although common in general sociology and sociology of education, has not been much talked about in music and music education. I describe some of those linguistic underpinnings in chapter 6.

Connecting Adorno to Weber

Explaining Adorno's concept of music as representative of the society within which it is created leads Martin to discuss the relationship between social and musical structures and music as social action. He concludes with what he calls the music business in a capitalist society, focusing on "the production of music in industrialized societies as a business rather than an art" (p. 217). Use of Max Weber's theory of the rational and social foundations of music allows Martin to place contemporary issues of music business, technology, and consumer behavior into a contemporary framework of bureaucratization and rationalization.

Small Group Discussion 4.4

How useful is it in your view to distinguish between commercial and aesthetic purposes of music? Where and how would such a distinction be beneficial in setting curricular goals and objectives?

Like Weber and Adorno, Martin does not hide his preference for a particular philosophical stance by which to explain "themes" in the sociology of music. Mostly grounded in Weber's theory of rationalization, however, Martin, unlike Adorno, accepts the commercialization of music, conceding that all music in a capitalistic society falls under the rules that govern that society. The so-called serious music scene of the classic tradition is part and parcel of commercial pressures at the same time that it is art. Likewise, the so-called commercial music (as defined by Adorno) has artistic merit when the songwriters and performers view themselves as artists. A sociology of music addresses both worlds.[2]

Key Points in Comparing the Texts and Their Relevance to Music Education

With the exception of Adorno and, to some extent, Weber, most music sociologists describe rather than make value judgments on what they see as good or bad, desirable or not desirable. They also acknowledge that, in order to be complete, such descriptions must be made from a macro *as well as* a micro perspective. In fact, DaSilva et al. include in their descriptions of musical behavior an interactive perspective as well.

Weber, Adorno, and Martin adopt specific philosophical positions to describe the origin and characteristics of different musics, audiences, and musical behaviors from a macro perspective. Weber and Adorno use those positions to make value judgments about what constitutes good music. Martin abstains from drawing such conclusions.

Adorno clearly contrasts art music that lies outside the purview of societal pressures and power structures from popular music that is fully controlled by the demands of the marketplace and the economic system of which it is a part. Martin, in contrast, applying Weber's theory of rationalization to his observations, views all music as the result of market pressures and economic power constellations.

Kaplan and Supičić come closest to providing texts of immediate relevance to thinking sociologically about music education practice. But only Kaplan gives credence to formal education as a significant social force in the way people are socialized toward musical values. He suggests providing a balance between the canon of accepted musical repertoire and the music the students know and interact with during nonschool hours.

---

[2] See also Denora, T. (2003). After Adorno: Rethinking music sociology. Cambridge: Cambridge University Press.

One might hypothesize that Weber and Adorno would be inclined to argue for the teaching of what often is referred to as the great works. Adorno would likely concur that learning to listen analytically to chamber music (preferably, the late Beethoven quartets or Schoenberg's late works) represents the most sophisticated form of music instruction. Other authors might suggest selecting examples from the history of music, both classical and popular, and compare them in performance and analysis. In all cases, music sociologists might emphasize that music teachers should be able to articulate the reason for specific curricular choices based on a theoretically informed position. Curriculum selections should be chosen for reasons that have clear musical, social, and educational relevance for specific target groups. At stake is if and how relevance and values fit together. Chapter 5 discusses some possible answers to this question.

Not everything in the sociology texts equally contributes to answers of what to include in the music curriculum. However, the texts provide a fitting framework within which specific topics germane to goals and objectives in music education should and can be discussed. Foremost among those points are, one, understanding the sociocultural and political climate that governs school curricula, a topic I discuss in Chapter 6, and two, continuing the debate and coming to some conclusion about what relevant music means in light of the different target groups that are part of music education.

Music as a Social Agent

Weber's framework, although situated in a theory of economics, declared the Western musical language superior because of its acoustic properties of sound. Indeed, the complexity of the harmonic possibilities inherent in tonal music itself has resulted in more than one musical style because the so-called Western (classical) musical style has become so malleable and pliable that it has turned into the basis for pop, rock, fusion, rap, salsa, and other musics of the world. The harmonic characteristics of Western music therefore have transcended any other style of music.

Other musical traditions, such as polyrhythms and polytonality present in musical cultures foreign to us, have often merged with the harmonic language of Western music. Weber's theory therefore gives support to those who believe that teaching the Western tonal and harmonic language of the past to all students provides us with the greatest arsenal of musical expression and social connectedness.

From a critical theorist's point of view, as espoused by Adorno and his immediate followers, the distinction between popular and art music lies in authenticity as the guiding principle for choosing appropriate repertoire. It is the justification for advocating world and ethnic musics in the curriculum because that music presumably has not been touched by mass media influences and technological manipulations. However, nearly all second- and third-generation critical theorists of today criticize this position, pointing to the social nature of music making and listening, integrally linked to today's means of communication that are, by necessity, mass media and technologies.

As persuasive as critical theorists are in today's world of scholarship, they are not the only ones to address issues of authenticity in musical works as a guide in making curricular decisions. Cultural theorists and ethnomusicologists with sociological interests have added their voices to those who talk about value education, educational relevance, and how musical meaning is determined. Clearly, no one answer satisfies everyone. But appreciating the range of answers might help one in selecting a solution befitting one's own situation.

DaSilva and his colleagues provided examples of different performance venues requiring differential behavior codes. The greater the diversity of musical styles and genres to which music teachers introduce their students and the more varied the times and places when and where such music was first composed and performed, the more one also has to consider the protocol of behaviors and social functions associated with music of different times and places.

A sociologically informed music teacher can learn what type of behavioral codes the students attach to different types of music: Does the music connect to their lives and experiences? If so, how? If not, why? Do the sounds (and/or text) convey exciting and aurally grabbing images? If so, what are they? If not, what is missing in the students' perspective? Can the students identify with what the composer wants to convey?

Receiving answers to these questions gives the teacher important insights into how the students think as they listen and perform. Those insights allow the teacher to predict reactions to newly selected pieces and to introduce repertoire in a way that corresponds to the students' way of thinking about and responding to music. It is a sociological way of dealing with musical issues.

Writing Project 4.1

Based on your knowledge of music history, develop some ideas of how music making in different performance venues of the past was accompanied by what DaSilva et al. call behavior codes. Determine relevant behavior codes of today's many different performance venues and compare them to those of the past. How fruitful and relevant for your own understanding of past musical traditions do you consider such comparisons?

As you consider the texts presented here, the close connection between philosophical and sociological thinking will become clear. This observation may become even more evident as you continue to become acquainted with other scholars not included in this overview who have thought extensively about the respective places of music and education in society. Often they come from different disciplines as well, be it sociology, musicology, ethnomusicology, or culture studies; general education, sociology of education, or educational sociology.

A distinction among these fields is at times difficult to make. This is so because of the fundamental similarity among the individuals who think sociologically about music, culture, and education. All of them step outside of their own discipline for the purpose of taking into consideration the multiple relationships that exist among music, different societal (social) groups, cultural values, and societal values at large.

Music education, too, is an interdisciplinary field and therefore draws not only from music and education but also from ethnomusicology, history, psychology, physiology, cultural theory, and, indeed, sociology. As music teachers reflect about their daily duties and work, their reflections have practical value if they help each teacher to understand, both from a macro and micro view, where school music fits into the larger scheme of education as a societal mandate, and the specifics of school politics created by daily interactions with colleagues and administrative superiors. The interactive viewpoint then connects both of those insights by helping each teacher to see his or her own role as musician and educator in what anthropologist Geertz (e.g. 1973) once called a "web of interactions."

Questions for Class Discussion

1. What benefits, if any, lie in distinguishing between process versus product when setting music educational goals?

2. Which of the books described in this chapter seem to speak to you the most and why?

3. What, in your view, does it mean to be culturally and musically educated? Do you agree with that distinction or do you believe both terms describe similar objectives? If so, what are they?

5

Musical Meaning
and Social Context
Thoughts by Selected Ethnomusicologists
and Cultural Theorists

Do not seek total equilibrium, you will not find it. Do not fear total
disequilibrium, it will not find you. Seek balance and live with both.

Introduction

Along with music sociologists, scholars in musicology and cultural theory also
have contributed to the debate on the relationship between sociocultural and musical values held by different social groups in society. From celebrating the American folk heritage to defending the traditions of Western classical music as the
standard of cultural values, the learned opinions and reasoned arguments among
ethnomusicologists generally derive from microsociological scholarship, whereas
cultural theorists tend to take macrosociological perspectives.

Following loosely the *Harvard Concise Dictionary of Music and Musicians*
(Randel, 1999) and what I found on the Internet for the term *ethno-musicology,* I
define ethnomusicologists as musician-scholars who study various musical traditions in relation to those traditions' geographic, racial, and cultural contexts.
Whether Charles Seeger studied the American folk heritage, John Blacking immersed himself in the culture of the Vendas in Africa, or Eileen Southern traced
the African American musical heritage from its beginnings to today, all three musicologists called attention to the musical conventions outside the mainstream of
Western classical music. They also placed those conventions into the larger
cultural conditions that shaped the societal group/tribe that engaged in particular
forms of music making under observation.

Cultural theorists in music are either social philosophers or sociologists
who write about the place of classical and popular music in society. They draw
from many different fields, among them anthropology, the arts, economics,
gender studies, philosophy, literary criticism, media studies, and the natural
and social sciences. These disciplines intersect with the field of cultural theory

because the construct of culture is a subject relevant to many different disciplines, not the arts alone.

Of the cultural theorists described in this chapter, two (John Shepherd and Christopher Small) acknowledge the social relativity of all human experiences, including aesthetic ones. It is an egalitarian viewpoint that gives equal weight to all musical experiences, regardless of their levels of musical sophistication. Susan McClary is included as a musicologist who "specializes in the cultural criticism of music, both the European canon and contemporary popular genres."[1]

A cultural theorist opposing all three such positions is Roger Scruton. He argues for cultivating the mind toward an appreciation of the dominant cultural inheritance that defines a nation's history. The purpose of such cultivation is to be set apart from and not to be confused with affirming one's social self through any activity that "is an identity-forming product of social interaction" (Scruton, 2000, p. 3). This type of musical culture is, indeed, diverse but because of its diversity does not contribute to a culturally elevated society, in Scruton's mind the purpose of education.

Music Between "culture" and "Culture": From Celebrating the American Folk Heritage and Popular Music to Rediscovering Grand Traditions

Drawing a distinction between a musically elevating culture and a musical culture that affirms one's social identity has caused some writers to separate *culture* (with a lowercase c) from *Culture* (capitalized). The c stands for what people do musically when living their daily lives. The other C stands for "high" culture. DeNora (2000) calls the everyday music of our lives "the little tradition," setting it apart from the "grand tradition" of music we call classical or art music today.

Scholars who look at the arts as reflective of "the grand tradition" often consider music a vehicle by which time-honored artistic and moral values can be passed on to the citizens of a nation-state from one generation to the next. The values are assumed to lie in the complexity of a composition itself. The "little tradition ('culture')" refers to people living and interacting with music in their spare time— while in the car, in the kitchen, or watching TV. The meaning attached to the music they hear comes primarily from the circumstances that surround an individual's lifestyle. Music is not the reason for being; rather, it accompanies life at a particular time and place.

The ethnomusicologists and cultural theorists to whom I refer in this chapter cast light, albeit in varying ways, on both traditions in relationship to each other and discuss the consequences of such coexistence for education. Lasting and changing musical as well as cultural values exist side by side in today's societies, and music teachers are called on to respond to those values when they make decisions about *what* to teach.

---

[1] http://www.humnet.ucla.edu/humnet/musicology/faculty-bios/mcclary.html, retrieved July 28, 2004

Getting to Know the American Folk Heritage: Charles Seeger

Together with his wife Ruth Crawford, Seeger (1886–1979) collected the songs they heard sung and played by rural Americans. Funded by public money during the depression, Seeger collected what one might call the music of the "forgotten" culture, American native folk songs. He interpreted that music as a vehicle of expression for people who otherwise were not heard.

Drawing from anthropology and philosophy as well as music, Seeger was as much a social activist as a musicologist and always argued for a close connection between the study of music and its social relevance to people. The legacy he left was a major song collection (e.g., Seeger, 1977, 1994) of what was then called "hillbilly" music, a forerunner of today's Country and Western music repertoire that has extended into much of today's rock and pop culture.

It was Seeger's conviction that "true" musicianship is defined by a thorough understanding of all "musics" in the culture of which one is a part, not just that of the European classical tradition. Unlike some other ethnomusicologists of his time, however, he also advised us to see the commonalities between musics of varying geographical regions and cultures rather than their differences.

Immersing Himself in a Foreign Culture: John Blacking

Born and raised in England, Blacking (1928–1990) began his formal studies at King's College, Cambridge, England (1950–1953), studying Malay culture and languages as well as music. Because of a job offer in South Africa, he stayed there for fifteen years, conducting extensive fieldwork on the Venda culture. He learned the language and immersed himself deeply in the culture itself, carefully documenting all of its aspects: the political structure, the economic system, kinship and marriage patterns, and ritual life.[2]

Blacking formulated what he called the cultural analysis of music, as distinguished from a musical analysis of music, because musical structures are a part of cultural patterns, the former growing out of the latter (Blacking, 1967). He thus highlighted the connections between the acquisition of musical skills and social skills where one is situated in the other. Best remembered for *How Musical Is Man?* (1973), the book reflects Blacking's belief that musical ability is a defining characteristic of being human, not a special trait reserved for talented individuals.

Blacking modeled an approach for informal music learning that occurs through cultural immersion. To immerse oneself in the study of instruments indigenous to a particular culture, be it African drums, Cuban steel drums, or Celtic harps, Irish fiddles, or American dulcimer, means to learn those instruments by rote. The same is true for learning to sing folk songs and ballads in the style in which they were traditionally passed on from generation to generation.

Acquiring musical skills through immersion and imitation rather than through music reading and formal, sequential instruction speaks to the difference between

---

[2] http://sapir.ukc.ac.uk.QUB/Introduction/I_Frame.html (retrieved from http://sapir.ukc.ac.uk. QUB/Introduction/I_Blacking.html August 4, 2004)

learning through living and learning through schooling. The first type of learning deals with a musical literacy that comes from a person's involvement in social situations requiring one "to pick up musical skills as the need arises." Musical meaning comes both from the music itself and from the social situation associated with performing that music.

The second type of music literacy is defined as the ability to read, write, and perform the notated score of a musical composition regardless of the social context in which such skills might be required. Although there is musical meaning in the piece itself, having its performance removed from the appropriate social context changes the experience.

African American Music in U.S. Culture: Eileen Southern

Generally regarded more as a music historian than an ethnomusicologist, Southern (1920–2002) transcended musicological research traditions by portraying and chronicling through ethnographic essays, articles, iconographies, and discographies the legacy of classical as well as popular music as it has defined African American musical culture. Her seminal work *The Music of Black Americans* (1971/1983/1997) deals with a rich musical tradition in the United States that should be known by all public school music teachers of today. As a comprehensive history of the African American heritage in and musical contributions to the United States, it spans the time frame from the 17th century to the late 20th century.

Beginning with the music of the homelands in West Africa, Southern introduces the reader to black music from the colonial era, eras of the revolutionary and civil wars to their respective post war years and up to the middle of the 20th century. Additionally, precursors of jazz are traced into the Jazz Age, and popular as well as classical music composers are described and documented.

The significance of Southern's book for music teachers lies in the systematically gathered information that teachers can use when teaching music of the African American heritage, a much needed component at least in required general music classes. Southern wove historical and musical with sociological constructs and thoughts, a useful approach for any teacher who wants to be broad based in his or her efforts to interest as many of the students as possible. Beyond that, Southern makes it easy to see how all music—classical, indigenous, and popular—can and should be looked at from both a musicological and a sociological perspective. One informs the other, and all three require context knowledge for fully discovering the musical meaning inherent in the pieces. This is in itself valuable learning that reaches beyond the discipline of music.

Whose Music?: John Shepherd

In 1977, cultural theorist Shepherd coauthored (together with Phil Berden, Graham Vulliamy, and Trevor Wishart) *Whose Music? A Sociology of Musical Languages*. The book reflects a social philosophy derived from critical theory and examines the choices of music in the culture of formal education and music education situated in a democratic society. The authors argue for valuing popular music for its own sociomusical sake, an issue relatively new in the United States at the time of the book's publication date. The issue was much more commonly accepted in Europe, especially in the United Kingdom, in part because of the way the music educational systems on both continents are configured.

Shepherd's second book, *Music as Social Text* (1991), articulates even more clearly than the first book that those who value art music seemingly only for its musical sake actually do so for its sociomusical value because the music they like is situated in a social context familiar and/or important to them. Therefore, people react to a particular piece of music not only because of the sounds themselves but also because of the situation in which they hear those sounds. It is what critical theorists and Marxists call *construction of meaning*, a term that indicates the active involvement in the making of meaning, rather than the extraction of meaning already present in a particular object. This viewpoint is similar to the one articulated by Alexander Baumgarten (1750/1758/1961) 250 years ago who had observed then that the same objects are perceived differently by people because of the experiences they bring to viewing the object.

Shepherd points out that musical meaning is derived from the interconnection between (1) what knowledge and experiences the listener brings to the social situation in which the music is heard, (2) what knowledge and experiences the listener associates with the piece itself, and (3) how both types of knowledge and experiences relate to each other, positively or negatively, at the moment the music is heard. He believes that music teachers should make these three points part of their instructional content because all three conditions together determine the meaning of any one given piece of music, be it a Beethoven symphony, a John Lennon song, or an Eminem rap. From a neo-Marxist educational philosophy, the complexity of the composition is of lesser consequences than the complexity of the social situation that creates a person's need to listen to one of these three choices (see also Shepherd & Wicke, 1997).

Musicking: Christopher Small

Small (1977/1996, 1998a, 1998b) takes a sociologically informed position about the "meaning" of music when he says that meaning is constructed as the result of the social interactions of music making itself. Taking a broad view of the term *music making*, he subsumes under the social act of music making the coming together of performing and/or listening. The meaning of music lies in the process of bringing the musical score to life by performing it. Consequently, Small finds the meaning of music in the act of singing, playing, listening, dancing, and/or composing. To show the interactive nature of this process in which all of the parties are equally involved, he coined the verb "to musick" (the 'k' is explained in his 1998 book *Musicking*).

Musicking (D) means that every time humans interact with each other through music, they are engaged in social relationships that also carry ritualistic meaning.

The meanings are constructed when one individual interacts with music alone or when several individuals make music together. Different performance settings and purposes create their own unique social and ritualistic meanings as long as time, place, and performance space differ. Both roles, that of the listener and that of the performer, are integral to those relationships. Both roles are active ones as one is defined by the other.

Focusing on the process of music making and listening rather than on what is being performed or listened to, Small suggests that the product-process dichotomy is one of the greatest distinctions between the Western classical music tradition and musical traditions found in indigenous music cultures elsewhere. It is, he believes, an unfortunate fact that schooling in the Western world "has worked to perpetuate those states of mind by which we see nature as a mere object for use, products as all-important regardless of the process by which they are obtained, and knowledge as an abstraction, existing 'out there,' independent of the experience of the knower" (p. 3).

For Small, the best form of music teaching lies in engaging students in informal music making in situations that are important to them. Overall, he takes a critical view of school music because it relies on established power relationships that often are detrimental to the celebratory and affirmative nature of the act of musicking itself. From his point of view, social and musical meanings should interconnect.

"Feminine Endings": Susan McClary

Susan McClary shares many of Small's thoughts but argues her case from the angle of a feminist musicologist. Most immediately, her role as coeditor in Richard Leppert's *Music and Society: The Politics of Composition, Performance and Reception* (1987) gave McClary the role of a critical musicologist who saw the intertwined connection between the social forces that shape even the most creative components in an artwork. Today, McClary is best known for her 1991 book, *Feminine Endings: Music, Gender and Sexuality*. In *Conventional Wisdom* (2000), McClary analyzes musical forms and their relationship to societal premises of "gender, narratives, and politics" rather than to music theoretical premises of "chords, forms, and pitch-class sets" (2000, p. 2).

She raises the question of how musical conventions reflect the social and political rhetoric of a given time and literally make those conventions "music to our ears." Like Shepherd and Small, McClary does not separate musical meanings from social meanings; one is imbedded in the other. The composed work itself reflects that connectedness.

McClary has earned a reputation for originality in the field of musicology by interpreting symphonies or popular songs alike as cultural artifacts, equally suitable for the traditions of music-theoretical and musicological analyses. She uses the traditions, through detailed description of how a work is put together, to "find what they reveal about the milieu that produced them."[3] Specifically, she focuses on "how

[3] http://www.ucla.edu/spotlight/archive/html_2001_2002/fac0502_mcclary.html retrieved August 4, 2004

music embodies shifting perceptions about gender and sexuality and expresses in subtle ways how individuals define themselves and experience emotion" (2000 p. 2).

McClary argues that music does not lose its value because its meaning is socially situated; in fact, it might become more meaningful if it is placed into the very center of human living and communication. To be a living human being means to be connected to and aware of the interactions among political, social, and cultural movements and motivations that shape us. Understanding that musical compositions actually reflect those connections can only enhance the meaningfulness of a work. Seen from this perspective, her thinking might be considered a counterpoint, or antithesis, to Max Weber's effort to elevate music to a level of rationality and mathematical purity that may not be there. Her observation is important as it questions the "natural" superiority of musical meaning inherent in Western classical sound structures.

An Activist on Behalf of High Culture: Roger Scruton

A self-declared conservative (e.g., Scruton, 1980, 2000), Scruton—British by birth—has taught both in Europe and the United States and considers himself an academic philosopher as well as a political activist. Like many other cultural theorists, he is a modern-time Renaissance man who writes as eloquently about architecture as he does about philosophy, aesthetics, culture, the arts, and music. His Web site lists him as a writer, philosopher, publisher, journalist, composer, editor, businessman, and broadcaster.[4]

Arguing for the preservation of the values passed on to a nation from generation to generation, he defends "culture in its higher and more critical form" (Scruton, 2000, p. x). He maintains that focusing on the individual as the exclusive standard of judging what is moral, right, and ethical in a society means to negate the community as the core of society.

In the preface to *An Intelligent Person's Guide to Modern Culture* (2000), Scruton states, "It is impossible to give a convincing defense of high culture to a person who has none" (p. x). As condescending as this statement may sound to some readers, Scruton argues with conviction for understanding the importance of high culture as the core of a curriculum threatened by a postmodern preference for popular communication over classic understanding.

He makes the case that society as a historically grown, social-political body is bonded together by symbols of knowledge shared over generations. Religion is one such symbol, music another. They, along with the other arts and literature, form the social capital of society, and it is the social capital that unites and educates. Formal education, therefore, provides "connectivity" between generations: "The rites and customs of a common culture close the gap between emotion and action: They tell people what to do, precisely on those situations where the ethical vision intrudes" (p. 14). And the rites and customs "legitimize not only the actions but the feelings that advance through them. It is easier to feel serious emotions,

---

[4] http://www.rogerscruton.com/rs-cv.html

when this is what society expects; easier still when provided with a repertoire of accepted gestures" (p. 14).

High culture, according to Scruton, is that repertoire of accepted gestures that holds us together as a community. Time-honored art and literature give us those gestures. Understanding them makes a community whole. It makes the community feel like one, an essential component of any society. However, feeling exists only "when it finds objective form, in words, gestures, plans and projects. A feeling involves a picture of the world and a stance towards it; it is predicated on understanding" (p. 16). The purpose of any formal education should lie in providing that understanding.

High culture "teaches us to live *as if* our lives mattered eternally" (p. 14). Like religion, it "addresses the question which science leaves unanswered: the question what to feel. The knowledge that it bestows on us is a knowledge not of facts nor of means but of ends: The most precious knowledge we have" (p. 17).

The reference to high culture as being linked to religion and religious meaning is purposeful. In fact, Scruton holds "that the point of being cultivated cannot, in the end, be explained without reference to the nature and value of religion" (p. x). Although he places the core of what he calls common culture in religion (p. 5), the core of high culture, he claims, lies in what Matthew Arnold called "the best that has been thought and said" (Arnold, 1869/1924, p. viii).

Shared value judgments are essential in holding a society together. To be shared, they have to be taught. Therefore, teaching those values should be at the core of all formal learning if the purpose of education is to instill in each student those values that define the best and most proven intellectual as well as creative assets of a society.

Philosophically, if one declares all thoughts to be of equal value, it downplays the importance of those principles that have held a society together for generations:

> If *any* text will do, then so will *no* text. Only if the texts are in some way self-selecting can an education be constructed from the art of reading them. Hence the need for a "canon" or tradition of literature. (Scruton, 2000, p. 20)

Curricular permissiveness, Scruton suggests, has resulted in a lack of ability by young people to make informed judgments about the ethical and moral standards holding a society together. School curricula, music included, should have the purpose of emphasizing long-lasting values rather than catering to the immediate needs of the students that can change at a moment's notice.

Scruton's voice counters the arguments of those cultural and critical theorists who, in the name of upholding democratic values, favor an egalitarian curriculum. At least one critical theorist, T. W. Adorno, would have likely agreed with him— certainly as far as music was concerned!

Scruton defends the point that music in the realm of high culture, along with the other arts and literature, stands for more than a social document of its time. As a symbol of collective thought and meaning, it represents aspects of a humanity that transcends any one composer's life. Therefore, valuing one's intimate knowledge of a Beethoven symphony is more important than knowing about Beethoven the person. It is the work, the score itself, that represents the values shared and cherished by those who preceded us. The score connects us to the past and is the reason for the need of music literacy.

The Sociological Significance of Arguments About Music Education as Value Education

For many years, music educators have found themselves in the midst of the debate over the place of music in the process of formal school experiences and the values people attach to music outside of school learning. The debate touches on (1) the difference between the musical values each of us, students and teachers alike, bring to the instructional process; (2) the culture we, the music teachers, are to represent and uphold; and (3) how music teachers and students can find a common ground of communication amid different meanings attached to or derived from listening to or performing musical works.

Sociologically, the answer we prefer is a reflection of our own values more so than of what is "right" for everybody at a particular time and in a defined space. Music teachers know this only too well because all teachers are most comfortable with teaching toward their own values and knowledge base. Nonetheless, they are expected to know the values and knowledge shared by groups of which music teachers are not a part.

In general terms, it might not be too difficult to ascertain what those values might be: All parents want their children to have a better life than they themselves had. "Better," however, depends on the specific needs of each family and is subject largely to each family's own socioeconomic circumstances. A teacher's personal viewpoint therefore cannot be the sole guide for deciding what constitutes a "good" society, be it economically, politically, socially, or culturally *as well as* musically.

Musically, perhaps Blacking is right that immersion through active involvement in the music of a culture, or subculture, is the best way to interact constructively with the people who are a part of that culture. If that is so, whose culture and/or subculture in our own society do we highlight? Should music teachers opt to focus on the music that forms the cultural core of the majority of students in a particular classroom? Should they highlight several subcultures within society? Or should they abstain from meeting their own students' musical cultures and introduce them to major world cultures as a way to broaden their horizons and introduce them to new musical and cultural traditions and value systems?

Like Blacking, Small suggests that music making must be process, not product driven. It should emphasize learning through doing and worry less about formal assessments of what is being learned. Ongoing participation in musical activities in and outside of school would provide the best chances for such musical learning. Small would argue that teachers should serve as facilitators for music making outside of formal school instruction, in after-school programs and municipal music schools, a model found more often in Europe and South America than in North

America. Its success relies on parental financing and support to a greater extent than many citizens in the United States are either willing to offer or able to afford.

The performance-driven music curricula in North American secondary schools suggest to me that music educators have made successful strides toward placing the act of music making at the center of all music schooling. In particular, musically successful students seem happy with what they learn in music as an elective. They acquire tangible skills in specific instruments or in voice and develop the discipline to practice and excel in those instruments. However, still somewhat lacking in the performance-oriented tradition of American music education is a systematic focus on individual and small group performances as an integral part of the curriculum. Although some teachers promote such activities, they are by no means standard practice across the United States.

Shepherd and other critical theorists like him question the educational and sociopolitical wisdom in continuing to promote a performance-driven model in which large ensembles are the norm. Participation in large ensembles inevitably promotes and favors a model of learning that operates from the "top down," being, by its very nature, autocratic. The model also stresses educational as well as musical values that are not easily reconciled with such goals as critical reflection and personal creativity (Keil & Feld, 1994; Regelski, 1998). Musical behaviors are conforming rather than divergent and contribute to cementing, not softening, extant power relationships between learners and teachers. Those power relations, however, affirm the status quo of societal values when the purpose of education, in the view of most critical theorists, should be to transform societal values.

Seen from this perspective, the question of whose values music teachers should or do affirm ceases to be a musical one as it enters into the realm of the purpose of formal education as a societal mandate. The next two chapters go into greater detail in that regard. At this point, it may suffice to point out the following:

1. The MENC National Standards provide music instructional guidelines for what to teach and such guidelines work for those teachers who have either chosen or have been instructed to follow them.

2. Kodály and Orff educators have found their answers of what to teach in the philosophies and methodologies that originated from ideas expressed many years ago. Other approaches spring up frequently and provide similar guidance to those teachers who are interested in going beyond any one instructional method or philosophy of teaching.

3. Ensemble directors who focus on participation in competitions and festivals teach toward repertoire prescribed by their elected colleagues and peers and thereby define the curricular content for their students.

Considering these three givens, it seems safe to say that most music teachers know what to do. What is lacking, perhaps, is a common rationale that places the *what* into a unified and agreed on framework of *why* we teach music as a part of compulsory education.

Small Group Discussion 5.1

Plan teaching strategies for a classroom setting of your choice that high-lights how "Culture" and "culture" interact in your students' lives.

Finding Commonality in Diverse Values

When we think about the viewpoints that different ethnomusicologists and cultural theorists have expressed about music education as value education, music teachers are asked to take a stand. This is difficult when we want to know and work with our students' values while we feel at the same time compelled to transmit cultural standards that have shaped our own thinking and being.

One possible way to work with the two worlds in tandem means to think dialectically. In fact, together with Jorgensen (1997, 2003), I believe that dialectic thinking can benefit music teachers in a very tangible way. To allow for seeming opposites to become the center of an action plan is a constructive and useful way of being proactive in the best sense of the word.

Practical Answers in the Dialectic of Opposites

Chances are that most teachers already live dialectically, always responding to and working with the polarities that shape their daily work. Teachers juggle students ready to learn with those who are not ready; they balance administrative demands for documenting learning gains by the entire class with pedagogical demands of individualizing learning for all students. Working with both goals knowingly and purposefully is the beginning of applying dialectic thinking to practice.

Music education as value education, seen from this perspective, means that students become enabled to discern, through performance and listening, differences in musical styles, origins, means of production, and intent. Classical music is not automatically good, popular music not automatically bad. The purpose of learning lies in discriminating both musical and social characteristics that render a piece of music valuable for reasons that include aesthetic ones but are not limited to them. To enable student learning in this direction, a music teacher's task lies in ascertaining (1) what meaning different students attach to a particular piece of music, (2) what social and musical values bring those meanings about, and (3) how students interpret musical choices as symbolic of their own cultural world, that of their teachers, or as one different from either.

When students express what they like or do not like about a particular piece of music, their statements should only form the beginning of the learning process. A dialogue should ensue in which the purposes and functions of different musics are compared to each other and each piece is being placed in its own ethnic context, time and place, yesterday and today. Such a dialogue can be a small part of a rehearsal or form the nucleus of a general music class, guided by such questions as these: For whom was the music written? Who performed it? Who actually heard it? Who performs it now? Who listens to it now?

The ramifications for such teaching practice are that music instruction can begin with the music-cultural framework with which the majority of the students in a class or performance group are familiar. Within the realm of performance, some teachers do not shy away from arranging familiar tunes, such as those heard as TV commercials, music excerpts from favorite films, favorite songs and melodies from the past and present. Other teachers may prefer to hold on to a more traditional performance model, still focusing on melodic material well known to the students. It may include patriotic songs, compositions that contain popular melodies, and arrangements of familiar ceremonial music.

Second, the teacher may introduce repertoire that is known primarily by first-generation immigrant students in class. This step is especially important in choral classes where making use of song texts in the minority students' first language(s) sets an important signal by the teacher that every cultural and ethnic background matters.

As a third step, the teacher may introduce the students to music traditions unfamiliar to nearly all students. This includes examples from the symphonic and operatic literature and can include the teacher's personal favorites. However, before taking this third step, the other two steps should have happened first.

The final, and perhaps most important, step may be to draw the students' attention to the multiplicity of performed styles and genres. This can happen through verbal dialogue but is more persuasive and powerful when the students become involved in planning a concert program and actually are asked to help in the preparation of the program notes.

In summary, as many students as possible should experience what it feels like to work with familiar-sounding musical material prior to facing musical challenges that are connected to the learning of unfamiliar sound idioms and structures. Such an approach does not negate the importance of standard classical repertoire in the curriculum but it also does not downplay the importance of playing and listening to music "of the people."

Questions for Class Discussion

1. How would you describe your own relationship to music *inside* and *outside* of school? How closely are both worlds connected in *your* life?

2. Develop arguments in support of Scruton's position that the purpose of schooling is to focus on teaching music from the perspective of "high culture" alone.

3. In light of the viewpoints outlined in this chapter, voice your own position and articulate your allegiance, if any, with one of the individuals introduced to you in this chapter. If you had a chance to visit with any of them, what would you like to comment on most immediately? What criticism or concerns would you voice?

6

Sociology of Education

Major Theories and Their Connection to School Practice

Celebrate complexity!

Introduction

School environments in which music teachers work are complex systems, influenced as much by political and educational policies as by budgetary concerns and specific dynamics within and between school administrators, teaching and support staff, and parental support groups, such as booster clubs and advisory boards. What do sociologists of education have to say about those institutional complexities that shape the school realities as perceived by principals and other school personnel?

This chapter and the next are guided by my belief that school music teachers should be familiar not only with the academic discourse of their colleagues in general education but also with the day-to-day concerns of their nonmusic peers and immediate superiors in the workplace. Being thus informed may benefit music teachers in their role as effective instructional staff members who share educational concerns that go beyond those of teaching music.

Presently, public school policies are geared toward (1) providing equal access to compulsory education for all children, (2) competing nationally and internationally with student achievements in math and the sciences, and (3) balancing local, state, and national control of other educational matters. Although not all such policies can be directly linked to sociological thinking, the latter has contributed to public debates on the purpose of education in society and on the sociocultural values schools should or do transmit from kindergarten onward. As such, sociologists of education have influenced educational discourse across the spectrum of teacher education programs, albeit to varying degrees.

The term **sociology of education (D)** first was introduced to readers in the United States in the late 1920s by Robert Cooley Angell (1899–1984). He and others like him held the view that a sociology of education has the purpose of describing scientifically what goes on in schools. Unlike Lester Frank Ward (1841–1913) one of the founding fathers of American sociology and John Dewey (1859–1952), Angell (1928) did not necessarily believe that scientific studies should or would lead to change. Instead, he saw a sociology of education as a vehicle of understanding the processes that govern educational institutions. Once those processes were understood, Angell believed, the need for change would become clear, in his view a necessary outcome of sociological analysis.

Fifty years ago, several sociological texts (e.g., Ashley, Cohen, & Slatter, 1969; Hansen & Gerstl, 1967) suggested distinguishing a sociology of education as introduced by Angell from educational sociology. The latter was to be viewed as a subdiscipline of education, whereas a sociology of education should be considered a subdiscipline of sociology. As suggested in Ashley et al. (1969), sociologists of education emphasize theoretical explorations; educational sociologists seek to improve instruction in tangible and practical ways by solving specific issues and concrete problems.

In more recent years, basic textbooks on the sociology of education seem to prefer the term *sociology of education,* downplaying any distinction between an applied and a theoretical field of sociology. Current sociological thinking therefore holds that theory should inform practice and practice should inform theory.

The Place of Education in Society: Selected Theories

By all accounts, Emile Durkheim (1858–1917) is considered the father of educational sociology. A professor of pedagogy at the Sorbonne in Paris, he first lectured on pedagogy and sociology in 1902. Already in 1883, Ward had argued that education as "a principal source of human progress and an agent of change . . . can foster moral commitment and cognitive development to better society" (Ballantine, 2001, p. 16). He and others like him viewed rational thinking as an essential skill for improving the processes that govern people's mores and ways of being. School education was considered essential in that regard. Dewey the father of what philosophically has been referred to as American pragmatism, expressed the same idea (e.g., Dewey, 1910/1933).

According to Ballantine (2001, p. 3), sociologists of education concern themselves with two major questions: (1) What is knowledge and how is it attained? (2) How do institutional settings impact learning? Specific to public school education, the first question can be answered sociologically only in the context of the second. Namely, one has to ask how school knowledge is attained and shaped by the institutional setting itself, and what the place and role of schools in a particular community is or should be.

In seeking answers to both questions, sociologists of different theoretical persuasion do share in some basic premises about how individuals become socialized to learn throughout their formative years. For example, all agree that our early years of socialization, that is, the years of our primary socialization, are shaped mostly by the influences of primary caregivers, be they our parents, grandparents, or guardians. Their norms and values, viewpoints, and behaviors serve as models for our own behaviors as young children. This is the case almost exclusively until we enter school, the beginning of our secondary socialization. Characterized by an increasingly larger influx of influences from the greater community in which we live, our secondary socialization is shaped by experiences that at times lie outside the purview of our primary caregivers and family.

Experiences provided by schools are one such source of secondary socialization experiences. But sociologists of education hold different viewpoints on the value, place, and function of schools in those experiences. **Functionalists (D)** maintain that school learning is the most efficient form of controlling and streamlining what societal values and accepted behaviors are being learned.

Conflict (or critical) theorists (D) give greater credence to the power of learning in context, stressing that skills and knowledge should be learned when a learner needs them, not when the curriculum mandates it. Schools should not only transmit knowledge but, instead, transform the learner by empowerment. Because critical theorists argue that school learning by its very structure cannot achieve such a goal, they do not consider it of equal benefit to all students.

Interactionists (D) take a position that actually combines the first two viewpoints by arguing that the greatest degree of school efficiency is reached when each learner is given the opportunity to learn at his or her own pace. As necessary societal institutions, schools are positive socialization agents only if they empower students to reach their own highest potential and aid them in constructing a reality that fits their own personal needs and aspirations.

Functionalist Theorists in Education

When Durkheim suggested placing pedagogical matters into a sociological framework, he did so for the purpose of making visible "the relationship between society and its institutions, all of which he believed were interdependent" (Ballantine, 2001, p. 7). This reflected Durkheim's belief that all parts within the educational process—the school, the community, society at large, and its institutions—have to function together to be effective, thus the term *functionalism*.

Accepting school learning as a necessary component of public life, functionalists in education identify each group in the educational system by the actions that set them apart from other groups. Students are defined by their actions as "learners," teachers by the action of instructing the students, and administrators by supervising the actions of the teachers. Although the actions of one group depend on those in other groups, their boundaries define them more than do the interactions.

To analyze mutually dependent groups in the system, functionalists determine how all groups contribute to the system as a whole. In particular, functionalists study how the different groups interact with each other in the system. For example, how similar or different is the teaching staff in beliefs and values from the administrative staff, how do the students interact with their teachers, and how do teachers and administrators communicate with the parents and the community? Are there any indicators of conflicts that potentially disturb the equilibrium of the system itself?

A functionalist assumes that each group in the system performs its role in predictable ways. The repeated observations of how the roles are carried out then become the data that form the scientific evidence for the rational argument of proposing change in the system.

Next to Durkheim, one of functionalism's best known early representatives was Talcott Parsons (1902–1979), who, akin to Max Weber, looked into all aspects that contribute to society's social stratification (e.g., 1937, 1951). Specifically, he distinguished between a person's *ascribed* and *achieved* social status.

In Parsons' terminology, one's ascribed social status is determined by who one is at birth by virtue of the socioeconomic class into which one is born and in which one is raised. Ascribed traits therefore are one's biological (hereditary) qualities, such as race and gender, and are non-negotiable. One's achieved status is the result of the roles each of us learns to assume in the various social groups of which we are a part throughout our lives.

In functionalists' terms, all socialization processes rely on an individual's submission to somewhat "prescribed and static expectations of behavior" that define the position one holds in a particular social group (Abercrombie, Hill, & Turner, 2000, p. 302). Not all social groups have equally strict and static expectations of behavior, but the social group of "young adolescents" does. It is, as James Coleman (1926–1995) first suggested during the 1960s, a society of its own.

"The Adolescent Society"

In two studies, now considered classic, Coleman documented the impact of schools with different socioeconomic profiles on adolescents' socialization processes. The first (Coleman, 1961) focused on the role of compulsory education in a young person's life. The second (Coleman, 1966) culminated in the so-called Coleman report, a study of the status of desegregation. Funded by the U.S. Department of Health, Education, and Welfare, Coleman compared opportunities and performance of minority students to those of white students.

The first study compared adolescents in 10 socioeconomically different high schools in the Chicago area during the 1955 school year. The purpose was to determine "the social life of the teenager and its impact on education" (1961, title page). Outlining his theory of the emergence of an adolescent subculture, Coleman described its power on the socialization of teenagers and young adults.

With data from extensive questionnaires and interviews, Coleman described the adolescent culture itself and the value climates of each school. The data also led him to propose the existence of "elites" that are divided into "local leaders" and "system leaders." He found gender differences in the adolescents' "paths to success" that he dichotomized as "sports or studies" and "beauty and brains."

From his findings, Coleman provided a portrait of the value systems among the adolescents under study and described how the adolescent society as a social system affected the students psychologically and scholastically, and secondary education as a part of the larger system of society. His conclusion pointed to secondary socialization as a phenomenon that, even though it plays itself out in the context of school, has a life of its own and is directly linked to society as a social system.

At the time the data for the so-called Coleman report (1966) were collected, most of the students attended segregated schools. Confirmed with repeated testing and based on information from approximately 5 percent of all schools in the United States, Coleman found that curriculum and facilities resulted in little difference in student achievement levels (Coleman, 1966, p. 104). Another finding was that minority students, with the exception of Asian Americans, "scored lower on tests at each level of schooling than did white students, and this disparity increased from the first to the twelfth grades."

This finding supported earlier calls for drastic and nationwide measures by which to achieve desegregation in an attempt to minimize the achievement gap between different races. One such measure was busing, the highly controversial and contested political effort to bring students of different races and economic backgrounds together in the same schools and classrooms. Coleman's work therefore is testimony to the close connection between educational policies and political mandates.

Small Group Discussion 6.1

Thinking about your family, determine in your own mind how you would describe your own *ascribed* and *achieved* social status. How might your own social status hinder or assist you in becoming a music teacher who is comfortable with communicating with students from backgrounds different than yours?

Conflict Theory in Education

Karl Marx and Max Weber are generally considered the most important forerunners of conflict theory in the field of education. The term conflict theory itself denotes that there is "a tension in society and its parts created by the competing interests of individuals and groups" (Ballantine, 2001, p. 12). This tension, viewed from a Marxist perspective, causes experiences of alienation between those who hold power and those who do not. As long as the prevailing class system contributes to organizational hierarchies that cement the status quo of societies rather than advocate change, the tension, or experience of conflict, remains. Once the tension gets too strong, change in the power structures occurs by force.

Early representatives of applying conflict theory to education were Ivan Illich (1926–2002), Paulo Freire (1921–1997), and sociolinguist Basil Bernstein (1924–2000). All three are often also referred to as critical pedagogues because they applied concepts of critical theory to examine the achievement gap observed by functionalists from the perspective of basic sociopolitical inequalities that are perpetuated by society and its educational institutions.

Pointing to the economic disparities between schools for the haves and have-nots, both Freire (e.g., 1968/1970/2000) and Illich (e.g., 1971) became advocates for the marginalized classes in all societies. Not only did they critique the unequal access to learning resources, but they also questioned the dependence society has created for all citizens by relying on schools as major socializing agents. Such dependence, Freire and Illich argued, leads to an ever-deeper gulf between what all members of society can constructively contribute without school knowledge and what they are allowed to contribute, once given permission by those who control the workforce.

Originally directed at societies in Latin America and other nonindustrialized nations throughout the world, Freire and Illich also included industrialized nations, such as the United States, in their criticism of schools becoming controlling social forces far beyond the mere acquisition of basic reading and writing skills. The emphasis on more and more formal learning, they argued, leads to a devaluing of informally gained, firsthand knowledge about how to maintain, fix, and possibly improve on the basic tools society needs to function at its most basic and essential levels. Therefore and contrary to how it was often interpreted, Illich's book *Deschooling Society* was not intended to argue for getting rid of schools but for understanding their relative merit in a society in which many useful and relevant skills can and are obtained outside of formal schooling. The issue is whether and how such skills lead to monetary and social recognition by a nation's citizens.

Bernstein's role as a major figure in critical pedagogy originated in his examination of how the social and power structures within which individuals live determine their opportunities for language learning, in his view the center of all learning and development (Bernstein, 1971–1975/2003, 1977, 1996). British by birth and upbringing, his sociolinguistic theory of class, power, language code, and human discourse in different social classes allowed him to analyze society from both the micro and the macro perspective of sociology.

The Power of Language as the Basis of Differential Learning Opportunities

People from different social classes engage in everyday conventions in different ways and therefore become socialized toward dissimilar values of learning. For example, a social convention typical of an upper-middle-class family may be to allow a child to argue with a parent as to why certain family rules are necessary. It is a convention not often found or allowed in families of Asian origin or in lower socioeconomic households.

The first scenario suggests language as a negotiating tool and source of empowerment. It equips the child, through verbal practice in real-life situations, to articulate verbally who he or she is socially. The second scenario occurs in social settings in which a child is not afforded the opportunity by a parent or primary caregiver to argue, question, or simply engage in discourse verbally for the sake of communication. Free discourse is replaced by reprimand or verbal directives, such as an order to do as told, a slap on the hand, or other means of corporal punishment. Language thus takes on a different function in the life of that child from early on. What constitutes a desirable family dialogue in the first situation is considered inappropriate behavior in the other. Language, similarly symbolic of power relationships in both cases, leads to different uses and interpretations of the power relations that do exist.

How children acquire their primary linguistic skills clearly leads to different abilities in as well as attitudes toward the spoken word as a tool in the learning process. This has ramifications for schooling that, with the exception of music instruction, physical education, and the visual arts, favors verbal discourse over nearly all other ways of learning. Schools thus inherently provide advantages for those learners who come from backgrounds in which the use of language as a tool of negotiation and empowerment is encouraged.

Consequences for the Classroom

Pedagogic discourse makes use of language that defines power relationships as well as boundaries of expected and accepted behaviors within any given subject matter. The curriculum and the language by which it is represented (i.e., *what* and *how* it is taught) define the knowledge valued by society. It is *valid* (Bernstein's term) in the eyes of those who control the educational processes.

In Western societies, most socioeconomically upward-bound adults of all races and ethnicities stress the importance of school knowledge because it is believed to guarantee a prosperous future for those who graduate from school with skills in math, science, and reading. But public schooling also includes the subjects of music and the other arts, sports, and the study of languages either as curricular, cocurricular or extracurricular offerings. They, too, become a part of the valued and valid knowledge sanctioned by society at large. As such, they fall under the rules that govern all aspects of schooling, aspects that include curriculum matters, teacher and student conduct, issues of classroom management, and communication.

A much-coveted communicative behavior in today's classrooms of the Western world is the verbal give-and-take between the teacher and the students as long as the teacher monitors the dialogue. Students not only are expected to play a particular role in the boundaries of such dialogue "routines" but also are assumed to know the boundaries that define verbal and nonverbal classroom discourse.

However, such discourse is the result of cultural and behavioral conventions not necessarily shared by students from different social classes with different knowledge bases. If certain cultural conventions are not overtly talked about in school, student awareness about them cannot be assumed.

The extent to which one does or does not understand educational givens within the context of school determines the degree to which the teaching process itself sends unintended messages that lead to *hidden learning* results. These can be positive, negative, or neutral. Bernstein called this component in instructional theory the **hidden curriculum (D),** a term that today is used in a number of different connotations.

Ranging from the meaning as Bernstein intended it, to "that which is not being taught" or that which "dumbs us down" (Gatto, 1992), the term covers a broad range of issues.[1] The root concern, however, lies in the assertion that formal education requires more than simple reforms to educate its young citizens in a way that truly benefits them individually.

Two of today's most noted critical pedagogues, Randall Collins and Pierre Bourdieu (1930–2002), point to the hidden curriculum as a persuasive and often negative force of learning. Collins (e.g., 1979, 1999, 2004) critiques standard principles of educational thinking as credentialism, suggesting that socioeconomic advantaged individuals reach higher-level positions because they get credit for where and who they are prior to having actually proven themselves. For example, children whose parents are doctors or lawyers are expected to do well in school because of their parents' social status in society. This expectation is the credit that propels them forward. It is the principle on which education as a societal system is not only founded but also perpetuated. Certain types of knowledge are valued over other types of knowledge. Having the so-called right kind of knowledge is rewarded academically. Socially advantaged individuals benefit from the system because they have been socialized toward possessing the right kind of knowledge prior to entering school. Credentialism therefore cements a system's status quo rather than propels opportunities for change. It is a criticism that has also been elaborated on by feminist scholars since at least the middle of the 20th century.

Bourdieu attacked the validity of formal schooling as it presented itself to him during his lifetime (see, for example, Bourdieu 1977, 1993; Bourdieu & Passeron, 1977; Bourdieu & Wacquant, 1992). Also referred to as reflexive sociology, the theory questions a system that teaches toward a cultural capital which is neither equally accessible nor shared by everyone in society. It affirms knowledge of publicly sanctioned art, music, theater, and literature without questioning its sociopolitical and economic roots. What Scruton argues for as the core of a child's formal education (see Chapter 5), Bourdieu questioned because that type of knowledge affirms the cultural haves and the power they hold in society.

Feminist research, too, has addressed the social and economic conditions that (1) declare certain knowledge to be cultural capital and other knowledge superfluous (see, for example, Hamilton & Werner, 2000), and (2) claim competitiveness in grades and achievement levels to be necessary components in all formal learning. Such claims, it is argued, are rooted in economic rather than pedagogical models that benefit each individual student equally (e.g., Aerni & McGoldrick, 1999; Dornbusch & Strober, 1988; see also M. Strober[2]). The well-being of the system itself, be it the economic system or the educational system, ranks above the welfare of the student. What is and what is not being taught as important information therefore should be scrutinized for its social, racial, and gender bias and reexamined in light of the multicultural and multiracial democracies of today.

---

[1] See also Gatto, J. (2005) Foreword by Thomas Moore *Dumbing us down. The hidden curriculum of compulsory schooling.* Gobriola Island, BC: New Society Publishers.

[2] http://www.stanford.edu/~myras/pdf_docs/fem_econ.pdf; retrieved December 2004.

Like Bourdieu, other critical pedagogues also view cultural capital as a commodity, not unlike economic or fiscal capital, that "can be traded in for higher status in school and later in the work force" and "allows students to reproduce their social class through family and schooling" (Ballantine, 2001, p. 15). The haves, already bringing cultural capital to the schooling process, favor what goes on in schools for obvious reasons and seek to convince the have-nots that they can share in the cultural capital by more and more schooling. It is in the interest of those in control of the curriculum to espouse its value as long as schools hold to a definition of cultural capital that favors certain knowledge over other knowledge and one social class over another. It is the same concept that Collins refers to as credentialism. At the heart of critical pedagogues' criticism of the educational system today is the inability or unwillingness of the haves to bring about fundamental change in the schooling process itself (see, for example, Giroux, 1983, 1988, 2004).

It appears that this criticism has proven to be of greater theoretical than practical importance to today's schools. There are educators, however, who, following the footsteps of critical pedagogues, have tried to bring about fundamental change by means of alternative schools and by models of thinking that seek to transform, not simply continue, educational practice in selected schools.

Conceptually, critical pedagogues of today primarily influence curriculum theory as taught in universities. It is here that their thoughts are juxtaposed with those held by functionalists and school practitioners. Most immediately, what functionalists and conflict/critical theorists in education have debated for decades might actually have had an indirect influence on what today is touted as critical thinking as a goal in education. Although it is not connected to critical theory, it received its impetus partially from theorists in education who argued for instilling in today's students a healthy dose of skepticism toward prevailing hierarchies of power and accepted belief systems in society. Critical theory, defined from this perspective, therefore is directed toward reflecting about and analyzing one's own role in the social system(s) of which one is a part. Its ultimate purpose lies "in self-emancipation from domination" (Abercromble, Hill, & Turner, 2000).

A second, perhaps less direct, influence of critical theorists on educational practice can be seen in the sociopolitical movement among some democracies, most notably that of the United States, to privatize education through home schooling and charter school options. This development seeks to move away from

---

Small Group Discussion 6.2

In thinking back to your own high school experiences (not necessarily in music), can you recall moments where "the hidden curriculum" became reality to *you*? How did it make you feel? Try to describe those emotions to one of your peers and see how he or she responds.

the principle of providing the same education for all because, in the eyes of the tax-paying public, the resources are distributed unevenly, a fact that bears directly on curricular decisions.

Interactionist Theory in Education

Charles Horton Cooley (1864–1929) and George Herbert Mead (1863–1947) are the two social philosophers/sociologists who must be credited with what later became known as the theory of interactionism. Cooley, a sociology professor at the University of Michigan, used the metaphor of what he called the "looking glass self" to describe how individuals interact with their environment. Mead, a social psychologist/philosopher at the University of Chicago, developed what he called "social behaviorism," a theory that later became known as symbolic interaction theory.

Both theories, later subsumed under the term **interactionism (D)**, grew out of pragmatism as a philosophical position articulated by Charles Sanders Peirce (1839–1914), William James (1842–1910), and John Dewey (1859–1952). All three believed in the importance of understanding the human organism in its relationship to its environment. Cooley and Mead shared that philosophy and used it to explain why, to understand the social structure of society at large, one must look conjointly at individual and group behaviors.

Cooley's "Looking Glass Self"

Cooley (1902) first described his theory of the "looking glass self" in *Human Nature and the Social Order*. He states, "The things to which we give names and which have a large place in reflective thought are almost always those which are impressed upon us by our contact with other people. Where there is no communication there can be no nomenclature and no developed thought" (p. 149). To think of the individual as being "apart from society is a palpable absurdity of which no one could be guilty who really saw it as a fact of life" (p. 150).

Cooley likened the "I," the self in each of us, "to the nucleus of a living cell, not altogether separate from the surrounding matter, out of which indeed it is formed, but more active and definitely organized" (p. 151). This means that a person expresses his or her sense of self through the presence of others: "There is no sense of 'I' . . . without its correlative sense of you, or he, or they. It is through the reference to the others that we define our own self."

Because of the "back-and-forth" by which we communicate with each other, Cooley proposed that "a social self . . . might be called the reflected or looking glass self" (p. 152). We feel or act in certain ways because we respond to the imagined effect of our own feelings or actions on others. More specifically, we act as we imagine others will act in response to our own envisioned actions. The social self, the "I" as the individual in a group, not only determines group behavior but, at the same time, is determined by it. Cooley referred to this social self in each person as the *empirical self,* a term developed further by Mead.

As an overall concept, Cooley's 'looking glass self' emphasized the social determination of the self (Legassé, 2001). This idea subsequently led to a better understanding of the impact of primary groups (the family, the play group, or the neighborhood) as important socializing agents in a person's development long before schooling occurs. It made the term *socialization* an educational household word, not only as it applied to primary groups but, later, to the process of secondary socialization. Most recently, the term has also been applied to how one becomes socialized as an adult. It often is referred to as tertiary socialization.

Mead's "Social Behaviorism"

Like Cooley, George Herbert Mead placed mind and self into the center of his philosophical/theoretical explorations of how people become who they are. Like Cooley, Mead explained the individual's mind and self as the result of a social process that begins at birth, the time at which communication begins. Thus the development of the mind is, from its onset, socially determined. Similar to Cooley, Mead worked with the notion of empirical selves, developing the idea further, however, by distinguishing between the "I" and the "me" in each of us.

The self is not merely a passive reflection of the generalized other but a complex communicative force. Only you know the "I" within you. As soon as you interact with another person for a particular purpose, your "me," your empirical self, actively responds. Which self is being activated depends on the purpose of the communication, be it the intimacy between two lovers, the role one holds as student in class, or the way one communicates with a parent.

You act and respond to your closest friend differently from the way you talk to a stranger; your role as a spouse is different from that of a sibling, a daughter, or a son. At times, the different empirical selves in you can be at odds with each other and may cause an inner conflict. Reality, therefore, "is not simply 'out there' . . . but is the outcome of the dynamic interrelation of organism and environment" (*The Internet Encyclopedia of Philosophy*, 2002, p. 8, paraphrasing Mead's *The Philosophy of the Act*, 1938, p. 218). Reality lies in your perception of the experiences your empirical selves have with the world around you.

Likewise, the way each of us communicates with others reflects how we see ourselves in relationship to those around us. This we show by means of *gestures:* how we dress; our preference for certain foods, music, which public venues we frequent; and, of course, our choice of words and body language.

Gestures can be verbal or nonverbal, clearly expressed or barely visible; in all cases, they are the signifiers of the meaning we attach to our surroundings. Depending on the context in which we communicate with others—neighbor, sibling, spouse, teacher, employee—we select from the repertoire of all possible gestures those we deem most appropriate for any given moment in which we interact with others. One acts as an empirical "self," specific to a particular role played in a

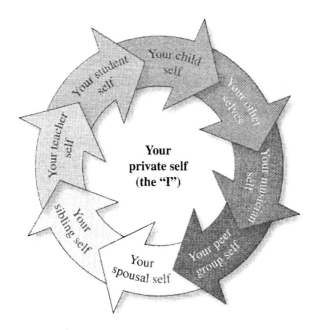

Figure 6.1 Mead's Theory of the "I" and the Empirical Selves
(or "me's")

particular social setting. Figure 6.1 depicts this relationship between the empirical selves and the private "I" in each of us.

It was Mead who first suggested the concept of both role taking and role playing as pivotal to understanding how we learn to interact with others from early childhood on. First we *take* the roles of father, mother, and teacher by "imaginatively" acting out the roles as we perceived them as being played out by the adults around us (Abercrombie et al., 2000, p. 301). Later those roles and their gestures become second nature to us and we become the roles; we *play* them in our daily discourse with other adults and children.

Small Group Discussion 6.3

As you think about the many roles you play as a family member, student in the university, and/or member in the workforce, what types of gestures are typical for each of the roles? Have you encountered conflicts between them? If so, how do you resolve them? If not, what is it that makes it possible for you to adjust to all required gestures with ease?

Symbolic and Social Interaction Theories Today

Later representatives of interaction theory were Herbert Blumer (1900–1987) and Erving Goffman (1922–1988). Both of them at one point were students at the University of Chicago, and Blumer was also one of Mead's students. It was he who termed Mead's theory symbolic interaction theory (Blumer, 1969/1986, 2004). Other sociologists and social psychologists refer to it as social interaction theory. The terms are now often used interchangeably, even though not all scholars condone such a practice.

Reviewing symbolic interactionism in different academic disciplines today, Charon (1998) stresses the construct of perspective as the vantage point from which we view not only our own discipline and work but also everything else. Only all possible perspectives taken together give us a glimpse at reality itself. Each perceived reality therefore is a relativistic, social construct rather than an absolute, objective fact. Described by Peter Berger and Thomas Luckmann in their landmark book *The Social Construction of Reality* (1967), this viewpoint is a social philosophy known as social constructivism or, simply, constructivism. Most symbolic interactionists use the term constructionism (see, e.g., Abercrombie et al., 2000, p. 320), a practice I prefer.

Constructionism in Education

Constructionism has been embraced by some educationists and educational psychologists and, more recently, by some academics in music education. However, those three groups trace their thinking less to Berger and Luckmann than to Lev Vygotksy (1896–1934), a Russian psychologist and psycholinguist. Like sociolinguist Bernstein in England, he emphasized the importance of language acquisition as the basis for how individuals develop socially and cognitively.

Constructionism in education is a sociocultural approach toward a psychology of learning that connects psychological constructs of learning to those of sociology and philosophy. Once again, the lines between disciplines become blurred. Constructionism is an interdisciplinary thought process.

Constructionists in education see schools as living, interactive "systems" that need to be analyzed ("deconstructed") not only as being embedded in the larger context of society but also as being shaped by the individuals who interact in the system itself. From this perspective, learners should be active participants in situations that require problem solving and critical thinking. The best way of achieving such a goal lies in activities students find relevant and engaging. This view mirrors Dewey's position that learning should be based on action and "doing" and placing educational experiences over those commonly associated with schooling.

In today's terms, students are to "construct" their own knowledge by (1) testing ideas and approaches based on their prior knowledge and experience, (2) applying these to a new situation, and (3) integrating the new knowledge into already formed ideas and familiar intellectual constructs. Music making, if placed into an environment of attentive listening and critical self-examination, fits this constructionist model.

In addition to constructionism in education, other interactive theories have sprung up as well. For the purpose of this overview, I single out reference group theory and labeling theory.

Reference Group Theory

Two of the founders of reference group theory were Robert K. Merton (1911–2003) and Tamotsu Shibutani. Both men contributed significantly to the question of how individuals interact with the many different groups of which they are a part (e.g., Merton, 1957, 1967; Shibutani, 1987). This includes how, at the micro level, each of us functions as a family member, classmate, spouse, colleague, peer, or friend. On the macro level, reference group theory addresses our association with larger societal groups, such as the socioeconomic class to which we belong; our racial, political, and religious affiliations; and profession and gender.

Because of distinguishing between each individual's connection to the larger societal structure through the groups of which he or she is a part, the theory has contributed to a clearer separation in the literature between a social group as a larger societal body and the groups of people we interact with every day, the reference group.

Bringing the macro and micro view together proves useful when one takes any one reference group and analyzes it further. For example, the social group "church" is, in effect, a conglomerate of reference groups, that is, many different subgroups within the larger group that makes up an entire church community. A school, too, is a social system with different reference groups, among which are, to name a few, the teaching, support and administrative staff.

Labeling Theory

Most recently, Cooley's notion of people's habit for wanting to label what they know has resulted in a new sociological theory actually called labeling theory (e.g., Hudak & Kihn, 2001). Words act as *labels* by which we infer meaning. What we call "knowing" really means having a word for an experience.

Linguists are well aware of this phenomenon when they point out that we give labels to objects as we use them. In fact, it was the impetus for Bernstein's work on language codes. The meaning of a word is not inherent in the object but in the function we attach to it as a result of our interaction with it. Educationally, it is an important idea because school instruction relies so heavily on verbal discourse, which eventually determines how well students do in formal learning.

Social Issues and the Nature of School Instruction

How do functionalism, conflict theory, and interaction theory with its various sub-theories illuminate the practical concerns that are at the forefront of school realities today? To answer this question, I again refer to Ballantine (2001), who pointed out five such practical concerns school communities talk about: (1) the place of parental involvement in schooling; (2) teaching style, technique, and classroom management; (3) establishing good relationships between schools and the communities in which they are located; (4) equal opportunities for learning and racial integration patterns in all instructional processes; and (5) schooling, employment opportunities, and the teacher as a force in the institutional setting of school. With the exception of the fifth item, which I addressed to some extent in Chapters 1 and 2 and also bring back in Chapter 7, I answer the other four under these headings:

- Acknowledging the presence of and need to reach an ethnically and racially diverse student body;
- Focusing on schools as transmitters of cultural values;
- Understanding the consequences of education and schooling as equally strong but separate forces in the learning process; and
- Teaching with knowledge of the power behind the hidden curriculum.

In dealing with these topics, I also include answers to other questions that today's public asks about the responsibilities of today's schools: the purpose of private and public schooling in general, the role of the teacher in what formerly was seen as parenting duties, and school as the place not only to provide after-school activities for teenagers but also sex education, drug counseling, and child care for the infants of adolescent mothers who try to complete their high school education (Ballantine, 2001).

Reaching an Ethnically and Racially Diverse Student Body

Most educational leaders see the system of schooling for what it is: a societal institution shaped by the same political and economic forces that impact all of society, dedicated to the dispensation of specific skills and knowledge valued by a body of experts. As changes in demographics and population stratification cause society as a whole to change, so do school policies.

Students of different ethnicity and cultural backgrounds bring diverse needs to the educational process, something schools cannot ignore. From a functionalist point of view, schools have to react, if for no other reason than to maintain the balance among all functioning parts of the system.

If teen pregnancies interfere with learning, schools must respond by providing help and support. If student violence in schools increases, metal detectors, crisis counselors, and after-school programs are a means to keep the system in balance. Changes in curricular options, course scheduling, and availability are options to which school personnel, administrators and teaching staff alike, have to learn to adjust. In all cases, corrections only establish equilibrium; they do not change the cause that led to the behaviors themselves and that upset the balance functionalists seek. Simultaneous with those functional changes also comes a call for greater parental involvement in the process of school education itself. Schools reach out to parents and communities to instill in them a sense of ownership and shared decision making that ultimately is hoped to transfer into positive learning behavior in the students.

Critical pedagogues and interactionists attribute the causes of specific student behavior to the way schooling itself takes place. Student violence, for example, is seen as the result, not the cause of, students being alienated from the educational process of which they are supposed to be a part. Students might view the formal knowledge they are supposed to acquire as irrelevant to their own social needs and contexts and therefore begin to act as outsiders to the system. Rather than calling the students "misfits" and "problem cases," critical pedagogues lay blame on the curriculum and the schooling process itself as the cause behind such "nonfunctional" conduct. Metal detectors, needed for the immediacy of the moment, do not correct the problem of student violence; they minimize it.

Neither critical pedagogues nor interactionists, including constructivists, have short-term hands-on solutions for school violence. Instead, they believe that structural and societal changes are needed that lead to smaller schools, significant curriculum changes (including, as proposed by critical pedagogues, fewer years of compulsory education), and new approaches toward instilling in students a desire to learn for life rather than for school. Goals aiming at the *transformation* of societal values rather than their *transmission* alone are at the center of such thinking.

Writing Project 6.1

"Think of three rather typical discipline problems during large ensemble rehearsals or general music classes and explain from the position of a functionlist, conflict theorist, and an interactonist why those problems might have occurred. Maintaining the same theoretical position chosen, describe how one could best deal with the resolution of such problems. In all cases, be specific about the grade level and circumstances of the scenarios you selected."

Schools as Transmitters of Cultural Values

Bourdieu and Passeron (1977) expressed the view that "all pedagogic action is, objectively, symbolic violence insofar as it is the imposition of a cultural arbitrary by an arbitrary power" (p. 5). Functionalists counter that very little of what good teachers do is arbitrary because the latter have to comply with societal "givens." Interactionists, too, accept schools as institutions in which certain standards of behavior, set by those "in power," are to be transmitted by the teachers and to be acquired by the students.

Interactionists understand the existence of formal education as a "gesture" of society, one that is as important as is voting and paying taxes. It is a requirement ("rite of passage") that modern societies have instituted as a vehicle for societal acculturation. It presupposes an agreed-upon value system that is shared by a very particular group of people within the hierarchy of social groups that make up society. Schools do serve as transmitters of agreed-upon knowledge; they become gatekeepers for social and cultural values.

In many Western industrialized democracies, the core values of what makes a "good life" in the eyes of many lie in material prosperity. It unites a diverse and heterogeneous society by focusing on each person's right to own a home and perhaps other property, being healthy, being free to come and go as one pleases, and being able to speak one's mind. Along with material prosperity, however, goes industrial prosperity, a goal that requires a workforce that contributes actively to the goals of material wealth and physical well-being.

As long as the citizens of a nation-state agree with those values and how to best achieve them, the purpose of schools in society continues to center on the acquisition of skills and knowledge that have the greatest potential of reaching those goals. All other values are derived from those goals. Historically, therefore, schools have focused on teaching skills of functional as well as mathematical and scientific literacy over other educational goals, a point often severely criticized by educators in the humanities and arts.

Critical pedagogues question the validity of educational values being derived from a market-driven economy. Such a practice, they assert, maintains the status quo of formal learning and negates what they perceive as society's obligation to narrow the extant gulf between those who participate in material wealth and those who do not. The fact that the gulf actually widens, they suggest, contributes to societal ills that result in greater poverty, alienation, and aggression. Simply continuing to transmit old values, as time proven as they may be, does not create the fundamental changes critical pedagogues believe to be needed in society as a whole.

Instead, the actual purpose of in-school education should be to free an individual's mind of conventions and static role behaviors that cement society as it is. Contributors to such mind-freeing learning are assumed to lie in divergent thinking skills and creative freedoms beyond the boundaries of accepted school learning. Assuming that schools, by their very nature, cannot deliver such instruction, critical pedagogy argues for alternative and new models of informal and formal learning that reduce the power of schools but increase the power of each individual in the learning process. One such alternative model is apprenticeship schooling while training for a trade under the supervision of a master tradesman.

Whereas critical pedagogues categorically question the feasibility of bringing old and new together in old forms of schooling, constructivists see a possibility for curricular changes in addressing the role teachers themselves play in the classroom. Rather than being seen as elongated arms of curriculum committees, test makers, and educational institutions, teachers should become empowered to make curricular decisions independently of such restraints. The reality of the classroom itself should determine what is being taught and how it is taught (e.g., Giroux, 1988).

Following this view, teaching "methods" are no longer at the center of teacher training programs as rules of "how to teach," but are replaced by reflection in action. This is an instructional model with which music teachers are familiar from one-on-one experiences in the music studio and from the way music directors conduct a rehearsal.

Acting and reacting to musical as well as educational needs as they occur in the moment of instruction, the teacher should possess mastery of the subject matter and knowledge of what each player (student) brings to the learning process and is capable of doing. Seen from this perspective, the teacher role becomes one that seeks to bridge school learning and learning outside of school. Hoping to reconcile primary and secondary socialization experiences in the students, the teacher may (1) show flexibility in working with all students, (2) want to know each student's place in the context of subject matter learning, and (3) use reasoning and context knowledge as necessary instructional tools.

In applying these skills, (music) teachers extend their roles as subject matter experts to include mentoring and parenting, roles with which many music teachers are already very familiar. With those extended roles also come extended responsibilities, which frequently makes teachers believe that they are, indeed, the students' surrogate parents or confidants. This is certainly true for the role many athletic as well as ensemble directors have taken on when coaching their students.

Education and Schooling as Equally Strong But Different Sources of Learning

Even though individual learning contexts differ from person to person, schools have to equalize differences in learning to some extent by formalizing and streamlining instructional processes. Referred to as *schooling,* this formalized process of learning results in intended as well as unintended forms of learning. Learning that occurs as an unintentional result of being engaged daily with one's environment falls under the term *education.*

The lines between education and schooling and formal and informal learning can be blurred or sharply drawn. Examples exist for all circumstances, especially if one also thinks of them in terms of intended and unintended learning results. The lines are positively blurred when a boy finds, for example, that the same names and music of composers familiar to him from home also are at the core of what is being taught and listened to in school. A less positive example of blurred lines between schooling and unintended learning is the little girl who begins to dislike "school music" because, in her perception, "All they do is 'ta-titi's.'" She disengages from school music because she does not connect rhythmic exercises with music making.

The lines between education and schooling become sharply drawn when what happens *in* school differs significantly from the experiences students have *outside of* school. This occurs in music, for example, when primary and secondary socialization experiences outside of school do not find acknowledgment in school. If critical pedagogues and interactionists are correct in asserting that valued knowledge is relative to who declares it to be so, students with musical preferences that lie outside of the canon of music literature taught in school can and may feel devalued.

To make up for the perception of being devalued, the resultant sense of being alienated from what goes on in class leads to misbehavior and, possibly, violent and aggressive actions. The behaviors indicate that the students found other ways of making themselves heard and "valued," even if negatively.

Teaching with Knowledge of the Power Behind the Hidden Curriculum

In many school subjects, today's educators do try to bring closer together informal and formal learning experiences and education and schooling. However, it is a matter of opinion whether the formality of schooling will ever be able to address the main concerns of critical pedagogues who point to the deep-seated problems associated with what is considered valued knowledge by those who hold the power to make sociopolitical and educational decisions.

On a less deep-seated level, however, a teacher's awareness of aspects connected with the hidden curriculum can impact some classroom management procedures, which, if unattended, might constitute a "hidden" learning culture for those students who have not yet been socialized to what schools expect of them. For example, next to the three R's of the formal curriculum (**R**eading, **W**riting, **A**rithmetic), there are the three 'Rs' of the hidden curriculum: **r**ules, **r**outines, and **r**egulations (Ballantine, 2001, p. 225; emphasis added). They describe what is assumed to be known by all students even though very few teachers spend time actually teaching toward these objectives.

Students whose primary socialization makes them familiar with the language of learning imbedded in what Bernstein called *valued knowledge* find it easy to embrace the knowledge teachers teach. This includes being comfortable with open debate, expressing opinions, and making general use of personal knowledge to give examples to clarify ideas.

To the extent that those instructional gestures match what has been part and parcel of the child's primary socialization process, the hidden curriculum affirms a person's values. The unspoken rules are familiar. Familiarity, however, increases self-confidence and enhances a student's sense of identity.

The hidden curriculum is likely to impact students negatively who, in Parsons's terms, place low on the axis of achieved and ascribed status. Such students might respond well to direct instruction that spells out clearly all expectations the teacher has for them, but any unspoken or unexplained rules governing a teacher's expectations of how the students are to interact with the teacher or classmates may result in insecurity and possibly a sense of alienation from the instructional process itself.

Or making instruction a competitive experience between classmates by using grading curves results in the unspoken learning that one person's gain is the other's loss, a cultural truth that may be in conflict with cultures that do not endorse individual success at the expense of one's peers or that value modesty over assertiveness (Adams, 1992). Even the often heard teacher order, "Look at me when I am talking to you" may have negative influences on students who have been taught at home to keep their heads down when an elder talks to them. They also may have been instructed not to respond to reprimands. In this case the students do not bring to their formal education the type of knowledge that is affirmed by instructional protocol. Instead, they bring another type of knowledge that is either not known by the teacher or ignored.

Seen from this perspective, keeping discipline in the classroom is no longer a pedagogical "aside" but central to the learning-teaching process. It contains challenges for both teacher and students alike, which, to be met constructively, require careful analysis and social vigilance. The teacher must consider *all* players in the situation, herself included, and not just the "trouble(d) kid."

This knowledge has found practical application in the many programs that exist to provide help and guidance through bilingual education for clearly identified minority students whose first language is not English. But, as critical pedagogues have pointed out, single-language environments, too, deal with differences in understanding and comprehension that can lead to differential student learning.

Seen from a multicultural perspective, linguistic and cultural conventions can be both: They can be barriers for as well as facilitators of learning. They are barriers for learning if teachers are unaware of how language and culture shape a student's identity. Different linguistic and behavioral codes defining the interactions with others at home and in the classroom, that is, how language is being used in different environments, leads to practical consequences for how students respond to schooling and formal learning.

Once a teacher knows that feeling ignored can be the source of many behavior problems, the need for knowing as much as possible about each student in one's class becomes paramount. This is one of the many reasons why schools call for increased parental involvement in the schooling process. It helps strengthen the relationship between teachers and parents and, thereby, brings the student's home world closer to what goes on in the classrooms. Especially schools with a culturally diverse student body benefit from regular teacher–parent contacts because the latter give teachers a better sense of the cultural dispositions and backgrounds their students bring to the table.

When teachers have learned to clearly and openly articulate, explain, and model expectations, rules of conduct, language, and etiquette of behavior commonly associated with school learning and the subject matter they teach, they become facilitators of learning. The process is a two-pronged instructional approach, in Adams's (1992) view a necessity in today's schools for teaching multiculturally. In fact, she believes it to be a 21st-century societal norm for instruction.

Adams urges today's teachers to become knowledgeable about the different cultural and schooling conventions with which their particular students are familiar. This may include some rudimentary awareness of the place and subcultures that form the background of the students' primary socialization.

Regardless of the national and political citizenship a child holds, the socialization experiences are always those the family provides. Those experiences and valued routines of behavior shape the students and what they bring with them to school learning. The coexistence of various valued routines of behaviors makes a classroom "multicultural." Once this awareness is firmly implanted in the consciousness of both the teacher and the students, we can proceed to teach toward a set of knowledge and skills in which all students can share. This means that, first, teachers get their students ready for learning and then help them explore, possibly at individually different rates, what there is to learn, uniting the students in a common set of knowledge and skills. By using this two-pronged approach, teachers may actually have a chance of also contributing to transformational learning.

Questions for Class Discussion

1. Discuss the pros and cons of functionalism, conflict, and interaction theory in dealing with explaining the status quo of public school education on the one hand and calling for major curricular reforms on the other.

2. Discuss the meaning of 'devaluing' a person. Give examples where that can happen during music instruction and find hypothetical solutions to such instances.

3. Describe the relative merits of constructivism as a perspective for music education practice and compare to it current practice as you know it.

7

Application of Sociological Constructs in Education to Music Schooling

Be careful what you teach; it may be learned.

Introduction

The social realities, outlined in Chapter 6, impact a teacher's daily work to varying degrees but are integral to all public schools. One, the achievement gap, first documented by Coleman, is real and a concern of all teachers, music teachers included. Aside from genetic differences that are not the subject of this book, music achievement gaps come about largely as the result of differences in formal and informal learning conditions inside and outside of school, which are precipitated by socioeconomic, racial, gender, and cultural differences in the students who either have to or elect to enroll in music classes.

Two, as educationists foresee the general student body becoming more diverse in terms of socioeconomic and sociocultural backgrounds, student familiarity with accepted traditions of "how things are done," once shared knowledge, must now be explicitly taught. This also applies to music classes, be they large ensembles or general music courses. Both consist of routines, rules, and regulations peculiar to music traditions steeped in mostly assumed (that is, hidden) rather than taught and articulated knowledge. To uncover such hidden "truths," music teachers may want to examine the origin of many of the time-honored traditions that govern so much of formal music schooling across the Western world.

Three, music learning and teaching are social acts at the same time that they deal with the aesthetics of performing musical works. Therefore, because social and aesthetic values go hand in hand in the moment of music-instructional interactions, questions about the why and what of music teaching remain philosophically as well as sociologically central issues in music education. For example, is there a unified set of *valued knowledge* in school music on which music educators can and do agree? If so, what is it? Does it help shape society into a unified cultural whole, as functionalists argue, or does it represent the kind of cultural capital that in the eyes of critical pedagogues holds back needed societal change?

Four, how music teachers respond to and act on the music education realities just outlined also defines their roles and identities as musicians and educators. To some extent, these issues opened the book. They also end it because a music teacher's role either as transmitter or as transformer of sociocultural values begins and ends with how music teachers see themselves and are seen by others within the complexities of school instructional realities.

Dealing with the Achievement Gap in Music: Bringing Together Informal and Formal Learning in Music

Many of the most well-known advocates for early music schooling, be they Shinichi Suzuki, Carl Orff, or Zoltán Kodály, knew of the power of informal music learning as a precursor to formal music instruction. Wanting to capitalize on what children brought to the formality of music lessons in terms of familiar songs and song games, all three musician-educators (as well as many others, too numerous to name) approached instruction by expanding and working with what the children already knew (had "in their heads").

As stated throughout this book, music, unlike some other subject areas in primary and secondary school curricula, has the advantage of being integral to our students' life outside of the school environment. It is an important form of knowledge (constructivists call it a form of knowing), of which music teachers can make full use today, just as Kodály, Orff, and Suzuki did almost eighty years ago.

Then, music educators talked about folk and ethnic songs as well as basic, "elemental" sounds; now, we talk about songs learned on children's TV shows, TV commercials, movie theme songs, and popular hits. Older students bring a musical knowing to the classroom gained in church choirs or community bands, by jamming in garage bands, and or by listening when attending concerts, watching TV, or playing their own CD collection in the privacy of their homes. The places and occasions for informal learning are, indeed, different from school, but the experience of learning is not necessarily less intense; in fact, for some students, usually such learning is more emotionally satisfying than what they experience in the formal setting of school music.

Campbell's (1998) documentation of the place of music and its meaning in children's lives during their first years of formal schooling provided evidence of five to nine years of learning, both formal and informal, that resulted in *knowing* music in a very personal way. Green (2001) observed about popular musicians that "[I]nformal music learning practices and formal music education are not mutually exclusive, but learners often draw upon or encounter aspects of both" (p. 59).

Informal music learning happens through voluntary immersion in a music-making culture. It is most akin to what John Blacking spoke about when he lived with the Vendas and fully immersed himself in their culture. Bringing learning through immersion into the context of formal schooling leads to what Dewey called "experimental logic." Applied to music, we focus and explore all aspects of our craft and artistry. Many music students crave this sort of learning, which is the reason why many of them want to become part of music conservatories, places that come closest to offering music study by a certain kind of immersion. It takes time but has the advantage of bringing together at one moment the need to know and the opportunity to learn. It allows for a person's transformation more so than any other form of learning.

What students choose as their favorite music outside of school depends to a large extent on early musical memories within their immediate family, their peer groups at various age levels, and their reverence of musician idols that often extends beyond the person alone to include his or her delivery style of words and sound. Body motions and performance mannerisms like those seen on TV and computer screen are as important in that regard as is a singer's vocal quality or an instrumentalist's playing style.

Especially older elementary-level students and teenagers look for connections between formal and informal learning through such clearly recognizable sociomusical behaviors and cultural symbols as what to wear, what music to listen to, and what movies to watch. Music teachers who know that their students make a difference between "life" as opposed to live music and school music understand that life music is used by young people to set moods, to send and share messages with others, and have fun. Life music allows one to "chillax;" school music tends to create an aura of being old-fashioned and "foreign."

Distinctions between life and school music cease to exist most easily in those students who get excited about and have the opportunity to learn an instrument in the safety of a group of peers. Therefore, instrumental ensembles can often bridge the gap between formal and informal musical learning almost from the moment when a student has opted to play an instrument. It is telling that the more successful students are usually those who also receive private music instruction and whose upbringing brought them in contact with the vocabulary commonly associated with school music.

Nonauditioned choral classes and general music as an elective require more attention than do auditioned ensembles to the differences between informal and formal musical knowledge that the students bring to the learning process. But the more a teacher keeps in mind young people's desire to learn a coveted craft and become engaged in an esteem-building group activity, the more powerful music can be as a tool in uniting students from diverse musical and sociocultural backgrounds. Especially if the teacher is open to performing music arrangements from popular movies and trendy songs, uses electronic sound equipment, TV cameras, and computer-generated sound sources as enhancers of otherwise traditional rehearsal settings, connections between the world of the teenager and the world of school music can be successfully made.

Learning a Coveted Craft

Learning to play an instrument is one of the most fundamental components in all of music and is a popular choice by nearly all children. The attraction of physically manipulating, exploring, and experimenting with the visible mechanics of a real instrument is immediate. This is true regardless of the music the students are asked to play, be it arrangements of African harvest songs, Indian reggaes, or excerpts from Haydn's "Surprise" symphony. The challenge of visibly manipulating an instrument even carries into the mechanics of making use of computer and MIDI technology to afford students the opportunity to "play with sounds," the precursor to making music.

Because it takes considerable emotional and musical maturity to understand the voice as an instrument, most children do not view their own voice as such. However, even though singing is not a substitute for the acquisition of instrumental skills, it should always accompany the study of an instrument, whether that instrument is an African tabla, a tambourine, a snare drum or other percussive nonpitched or pitched instruments, the electronic keyboard, the guitar, standard brass, wind, or string instruments.

Sociologically, the more music teachers base the music curriculum on the development of the craft of playing a musical instrument, the more learning reaches beyond the formality of schooling alone. It touches on a child's desire to experiment with new skills and to explore sounds and sights. Therefore, if channeled and guided correctly, learning an instrument even in the formal context of schooling can foster emotional involvement and personal curiosity in the students, just as it would as the result of informal learning outside of school.

This fact speaks against critical pedagogues' assertion that *all* formal schooling stifles curiosity, a desire to experiment, and personal involvement in learning. Their assertion turns true only if students' musical capabilities and the challenges imposed on them by their teachers do not match, a fact fully explored philosophically by Elliott (1995) as well as Woodford (2005) and pedagogically most recently by Regelski (2004).

If the study of music is situated in and derived from the learning of an instrument as just described, the very factor of control inherent in formal instruction may actually be its strength. As long as all students are given choices and opportunities to learn at paces appropriate for their social and musical maturity, the prospect of playing an instrument generally invites curiosity and excitement.

Finding and responding to each student's social and musical maturity might also call for the teaching of music in smaller ensembles, grouped according to ability and musical interests. Although making room for small ensemble classes can run into organizational, financial, and scheduling problems, it should be considered a necessary instructional adjustment in light of today students' learning needs. But even as music teachers become successful in diversifying and individualizing their programs, regularly combining students into larger ensembles is likely to remain one of the most visible sociomusical backbones of American music schooling.

The Large Ensemble as an Important Component in Public School Music

For the U.S. public, the most visible and expected gesture of music schooling is the band playing for and during ball games. Student participation in such events connects the formal world of school with the much-coveted world of entertainment and community involvement. The craft of playing an instrument is put to immediate and functional use for the entire school community to see and hear. Being in the public eyes and ears is an essential component of what secondary-level school music is about.

Efforts by general music specialists to work toward similar goals of public visibility are just as important. However, those efforts tend to result less in concert-like events but more in open displays of learning in progress. Often scheduled during open house or PTA meetings, such displays may range anywhere from public demonstrations of rhythmic drumming and solfège exercises to the viewing of listening maps or "found sound" compositions. The purpose is that attending parents witness the learning progress of their children.

In all cases, whether it is a highly polished concert by the top ensembles or a showcase of solfège exercises by all second graders of a particular school, public performances bring together the school community, parents, and interested public for more than musical reasons. Developing and buttressing school spirit, reinforcing enthusiasm for formal learning, and sharing in other common values, including musical ones, are the main goals during such musical gatherings. For the music teacher, of course, the main reason is to bring beautiful music to the attention of the public, hoping thereby to make a case for the importance of music in the students' lives.

All of the purposes, goals, and hopes taken together define the importance of the musical event itself. The meaning parents attach to a choral concert or a *music class* demonstration during an open house is as important as are the hopes a music teacher has for an ensemble to do well in contest. No one value should top the other; all coexist as the result of experiences, both formal and informal, that each individual brings to a particular event. Social and musical values interact with each other.

A principal may not hear that the band plays in tune during a concert fully devoted to Civil War music. But he knows that the auditorium is filled with enthusiastically applauding families who may have many reasons to do so, ranging from loving to watch the energy and spirit with which the students play their instruments to remembering one's own school days, admiring the costumes in which the students perform, or enjoying the poetry recited in between songs by other teachers.

Not everyone who attends a concert knows how much work goes into the preparation musically, but everyone realizes that what is being witnessed is a schoolwide event, something that transcends music as a school subject. It becomes a community event and merges life inside and outside of school. Pedagogically, concerts are the culminating point of music instructional processes. From a

---

Observation Project 7.1

Attend a school concert in your neighborhood and take note of the way the program is structured. How varied is the music? How does the audience respond? How involved are the performing students?

---

sociological perspective, public displays of musical learning in the form of concerts and showcasing student learning are pivotal to music as a part of the school curriculum.

If one defines a concert as the public display of music making, all school music programs should be characterized by them. Apart from the typical, traditional seasonal concerts schools regularly offer, additional public performances may display individual students' talents and group compositional projects. They may include community sing-alongs and joint cultural/musical events between several schools. Thematically structured, they may celebrate all of the arts in school or feature other subject matter areas through student-composed as well as student-performed songs, poetry, and instrumental pieces.

Once music teachers accept that many values, musical and nonmusical, aesthetic and social, define a successful music program in the eyes of the public, a teacher may want to use that knowledge as a guide for programming and planning performances that appeal to the varied tastes school audiences customarily represent. Recognizing the variety of musical preferences and cultural traditions, musical selections should audibly represent that variety.

The Hidden Curriculum in School Music

The diversity of musical preferences and cultural traditions also lies at the center of understanding that certain musical conventions and valued behaviors, shared by musicians but often left unexplained and unquestioned, can create learning barriers among students who have little or no musical background. A second, more deep-seated and perhaps philosophically more challenging viewpoint is that espoused by critical pedagogues and constructionists. They question, for example, the large ensemble tradition as a positive model for today's music education because the teacher-conductor as the sole holder of social as well as musical power may inhibit creativity and musical inquisitiveness in the students. Both issues, musical conventions and valued behaviors as barriers of learning as well as deep-seated criticisms of standard formal music making in Western societies, require attention.

Musical Conventions and Valued Behaviors as Barriers of Learning

Musical conventions and behaviors, fully accepted as appropriate cultural gestures by the world of musicians, become rules, routines, and regulations in the

---

The Dress Rehearsal (Classroom Scenario 7.1)

A seventh-grade choir gives its first public performance during the annual spring choral concert. The director tells the girls to show up in time for dress rehearsal. Carol, very anxiously and seemingly embarrassed, raises her hand and says that there is no way she can make it in time because she will not have time to change between the previous class and the time the rehearsal begins. Some girls giggle; others agree with Carol. At first, the teacher thinks that Carol is trying to act up and is about to say so. But he suddenly realizes that he has never explained to the girls the meaning of "dress rehearsal." He does so and assures Carol that it was good for her to speak up.

---

eyes of the nonmusician that sometimes appear to be the essence of music itself. Such conventions often are imbedded in musical terminology or related to concert etiquette: What are "movements" in classical instrumental music? How do we know when to clap during a concert? Why do jazz concerts have a different etiquette for applause than classical concerts? What is the difference between a song and a "piece of music"? Why is one person a composer and the other a songwriter? Why do classical radio stations give details about opus numbers and keys when this is not done for popular music? Where do these different standards come from, and how important are they?

Musicians know that these are seemingly tangential questions to the essence of understanding music. The questions describe sociomusical gestures with which we, the musicians, have become comfortable as the result of years of socialization. In fact, the gestures have become such a part of us that we are not even aware that so many nonmusicians, students included, feel intimidated by the behaviors associated with those gestures and interpret them as the essence of knowing classical music.

Students with prior formal musical instruction generally are at an advantage over students who rely entirely on music instruction in school. This is where the cultural capital criticized by critical theorists comes in. It represents an educational inequity with which many music teachers struggle.

Formal music study outside of school provides a student with an almost serendipitously gained knowledge of musical conventions. The conventions include performance etiquette, how and when to interact with other members of the ensemble, developing practice routines that exceed simply repeating an entire song over and over, and feeling at ease with doing what the teacher asks one to do. Names of specific instruments as well as composers become more easily part of one's language repertoire; terminology, such as what it means to be "in tune," becomes second nature to one group of students although it remains somewhat "academic" to another group. Even the teacher's role as conductor/director may

---

Feeling Left Out (Classroom Scenario 7.2)

A beginning band class works on three different exercises in preparation for learning by rote the first phrase of Beethoven's "Ode to Joy." Based on the response of some of the students, the teacher assumes that the students are familiar with the melody. Indeed, some students already know the entire melody from church and therefore find it quite easy to figure out the fingering on their instruments. Bob, however, neither knows the melody nor its title. He seems fidgety and unsure of himself. Eventually, watching the others, he copies what they are doing. But in doing so, he feels ignorant and frustrated, an outsider against those who "know." He begins to think of himself as a "musical outsider" and wonders whether joining the band was the right decision.

---

require some clarification because other than having watched their hometown marching band on Friday evenings, many students may have never experienced the formality involved in attending a live professional symphony orchestra or chamber ensemble.

As terminology, rules, and expected behaviors governing musical conventions differ for the music worlds of which our students and we are a part, we must be cautious about assumed givens in the music classroom. For example, rules of ensemble seating and chair placement as well as the resultant section dynamics and hierarchies within and across sections are known realities among musicians.

Musicians know, for instance, that percussionists in the back of the ensemble are not less important than a clarinetist sitting in the first row. But their positioning is a musical convention that brings with it particular pedagogical challenges for the teacher, especially in a junior high band setting. The distance between the percussion section and the teacher makes it difficult to keep discipline among the group. The need to raise one's voice can make the teacher sound angry, a trait that then gets interpreted by the students as the teacher picking on the percussionists. Young students need to be taught early on how an ensemble is structured and why and what responsibilities go along with such structure. Or the teacher may decide not to follow the traditional seating arrangement but to place the percussionists directly in front.

Inexperienced choristers, too, are not immune from assumed rather than taught knowledge. Often based on their experiences in choir settings at their place of worship, students may know how choirs act within a worship service, knowledge that differs considerably, of course, between denominations. But school choirs do operate in formats whose traditions are as variable as the types of choirs that exist. At times akin to the discipline in an instrumental ensemble, choral protocol, such as warming-up exercises, singing a song in solfège before singing the actual words, are assumed normal routines by the music teacher but may be unfamiliar to many students and actually can make the learning harder (as is often the case for untrained choral singers who find it easier to use the words rather than sol-fa syllables as a guideline for reading the music).

Or, when joining a band, not all students know offhand all instruments by name and function. Students generally are also unfamiliar with the composers of the pieces they perform. Other expected knowledge includes the skill of listening to each other, keeping eye contact with the conductor, and marking one's score for identifying troublesome places. These are skills that must be taught if they are to become formally learned and used knowledge.

It is an accepted behavior in the professional music world that, during rehearsal, conductors are short and direct in their verbal comments, keep praises to a minimum, and are focused more on the music than on those who make it. For some students, such focus can be disconcerting when they perceive a difference between the way the teacher acts off the podium and on it. Being musically concentrated and focused can come across to the students as standoffish. Not all students know how to interpret such demeanor in the correct context. If it remains unexplained, even the most accepted conventions of musical behaviors can therefore become barriers of learning.

One of the greater challenges that lie hidden behind the official curriculum is knowing the reason for which music is taught in the schools. For example: It is festival time. The students have worked hard on the three pieces they are to have ready for performance. On the wall hangs a banner that says:

EVERYTHING FOR THE ENSEMBLE, NOTHING FOR THE INDIVIDUAL!

The teacher tells the students how hard work will pay off if they just practice a little harder at home and how the benefit of the whole group relies on each person's efforts. The students are highly motivated, wanting to please themselves and their teacher. They practice outside of class and feel ready when the day of performance arrives. In his final motivational speech to the ensemble, the teacher reiterates that hard work always pays off and that he expects nothing but the best from the students. Alas, their contest rating ends up being a 2, not the anticipated 1!

The disappointment is clearly visible in everybody's face, including that of the teacher, even though he tries to cheer up the students by saying they could not have done any better. Chris, a quiet student normally, speaks up and says, "If hard work does not pay off, why do we do it?" Responds Katy, "Because if we had made a 1, we would *really* be good."

Covertly learned in this class is that school music means to submit to goals beyond one's own control and that the rewards lie in competing with the abilities of others rather than one's own. In the nomenclature of some professional schools, one would call it survival of the musically fittest! Not rewarded under such a slogan is the experience of engaging in hard work for its own sake and for the sake of enjoying the pleasure of musical and artistic immersion.

By focusing on the musically fittest, many school music programs today tailor themselves after the way professional schools operate. Although this approach

---

Small Group Discussion 7.1

1. Discuss the two highlighted scenarios as possible sources for disruptive behavior problems during class as well as possible long-term learning effects.
2. Find other examples from personal or shared experiences.
3. Examine the place of competitions in the world of music learning. Where is competitive behavior appropriate and where does it inhibit learning?

---

may have merit in the professional world, one must wonder whether the same principle should also be the underlying message, the hidden code, of music as an elective school subject. Perhaps critical pedagogues are right when they admonish educationists to reexamine the place of competitiveness in the world of learning.

The assumption of large ensembles as the sociomusical backbone of American music education has its critics because of the aforementioned downgrading of the individual player as a number in a larger group effort. In fact, how often do ensemble directors think in terms of their clarinets, saxophones, altos, or tenors rather than in terms of the students themselves and their individual musical aspirations? Performing a musical work does require technical precision and musical sensitivity of each of our students, but do we actively engage them as musical individuals in actual decision-making processes connected to interpretative approaches and creative decisions?

The role of the teacher as predominantly a conductor has been brought into question by critical pedagogues and constructionists alike as they point to the conductor's unlimited control and power over the students and the replication of the musical work. In large ensembles, individual players relinquish musical control. But unlike professional musicians, students do not know why certain musical decisions are being made. Furthermore, the exclusive focus on replication of existing works rather than on the creation of new ones implies that music composition lies outside the realm of formally learning music.

Composing and engaging in improvisatory tasks are not ranked high either on the agenda of most successful ensemble teachers or in the minds of most musicians, most likely because musicians themselves feel ill equipped to teach either. Developing one's musical imagination appears to be viewed as a form of knowledge reserved for those "with talent." It is the same kind of wording the general public uses when talking about the ability to play a musical instrument! It is a myth that permeates music curricula in the United States from kindergarten to college because it is inadvertently upheld by omitting compositional activities as an integral part of all music instruction.

Finally, the most deep-seated consequences of the hidden curriculum in music may lie in (1) the relative weight music as a subject receives by the school and general public, (2) how musical learning is rewarded in terms of grades, ratings, and competitive audition processes that weed out students for purposes of ensemble efficiency or a teacher's own convenience, and (3) how and why instruments are assigned to certain students and not to others. The hidden curriculum in music therefore has to do with accepting existing economic and socioculturally conditions as inevitable rather than understanding that they are socially constructed realities, changeable once we embark on rethinking the purpose of schooling and education in general. These and related issues have been comprehensively described for music education by, among others, Lamb, Dolloff, and Howe (2002) and O'Toole (1997a, 1997b, 1998).

Musical Skills and Knowledge as Cultural Capital

In the current reality of public schools, a musically educated student graduating from an American high school plays at least one instrument and/or sings at an acceptable level of technical ability, can read musical notation to some extent, and has participated successfully in numerous music festivals and performance contests. These are the musical knowledge and skills that presently determine musically what Bernstein called *valued knowledge,* what Scruton hails, and what Bourdieu critiques as *cultural capital.* Relative to music, one might refer to it as musical capital.

What is that capital? Most immediately it falls under what music experts call *musicianship,* a term that is broad in its meaning. Like the term *literacy* in language arts, musicianship consists of multifaceted traits and skills. In the United States, many of those skills and knowledge have been defined in the National Association for Music Education (MENC) state-level standards. They include performance skills, the ability to read music at sight as well as improvisatory abilities, analytical skills by which to discern different musical styles and genres not only from the Western classical repertoire but also from non-Western musical traditions.

Are those abilities and skills a means of building a lifelong involvement with music, and does such an involvement cement, as Bourdieu would argue, the status quo of musical doing? The answer, I believe, derives from the significance that teachers attach to the musicianship their students bring to the formal learning experience and the craft of learning to play an instrument.

As with all knowledge, musicianship depends on context and place (Kincheloe & Pinar, 1991). It is imbedded in a student's prior musical knowledge, what students want to learn, and the school setting within which that learning takes place. Music as a compulsory subject aims at a different form of musicianship than does music as an elective. Also, geographical locations and sociocultural conditions of the communities within which schools are located impact the ease and pace at which teachers can reach any of the officially declared musical standards of musicianship as declared by the experts.

Music as a Compulsory Subject

The diversity of the student body in compulsory music classes demands an instructional approach that is different from what happens when a student later chooses to enroll in school ensembles or in a course called general music. Therefore, the musical experiences in one context should not merely become a watered-down version of the other, and compulsory classes should not exclusively serve as the stepping-stone for music as an elective in the later school years. Instructional purposes and settings need to match.

For the general music student, especially for those from third grade on, the use of various strategies, such as the study of nontraditional instruments, different forms of drumming, and skill development on the electronic keyboard, can enhance multicultural teaching and learning processes. Because computer-generated sounds are among the valued musical sounds of the younger generations, available software is another avenue by which students can learn to manipulate and string together sounds according to specified musical rules. All of these opportunities require craftsmanship that represents true cultural capital in that it equips a student with new and desired skills.

Through those skills, including those of developing basic instrumental dexterity, the training of aural and rhythmic acuity should become the core of the general music curriculum. Such aural literacy is less concerned with a person's ability to notate the sounds or reproduce them from a written score than with having the sounds in one's head, being able to recall them for purposes of playing with them, manipulating them, recording and rearranging them in many different forms. Such music inevitably begins with musical patterns and melodic material with which the student is familiar. By encouraging the student to change and alter those patterns, the student's musical horizon gets broadened and primed for listening to unfamiliar musical material.

Listening tasks are most successful if they are connected to the playing of song excerpts or melodic patterns imbedded in the music to be listened to, regardless of the musical choices themselves. Listening to renditions of different musical traditions should be done for the purpose of drawing comparisons between and working with diverse forms of musical expression, functions, and uses.

All music is ethnic music, to someone. It is the essence of teaching multiculturally. Knowing about differences in musical conventions and functions becomes the center of what students take away from such instruction. Both the development of comparative listening skills and the opportunities to develop firsthand knowledge of performance and improvisatory skills at the most basic level can become *valued skills* not because they confirm the values of a particular social class but because each individual student who attended the music class has new skills.

Music as an Elective

As alluded to earlier, in many parts of the United States formal music study at the secondary level of schooling already focuses on the development of performance skills. This is especially true for students who have elected to enroll in band, choir, and string/orchestra programs. Not only are those programs structured according to levels of abilities, but some schools also allow auditioned ensembles in which the most talented students advance most rapidly.

Depending on school size and program, the best performers often have the chance to enroll in music theory and/or music history, frequently in preparation for college-level music study. Successful music students therefore are becoming most easily socialized toward the musical values that shape the *valued knowledge* shared by trained musicians.

Students who either do not meet the audition requirements set by music teachers or who attend schools without tiered ensemble options other than band are often assigned to what is called "general music," "music appreciation," or nonauditioned choirs. Not surprisingly, it is in these classes that teachers encounter the greatest disciplinary problems because the students' musical interests are not easily accommodated.

Adolescents tend to be articulate about their own needs and motivations and are very aware of the differences between real-life learning and school learning. The musical and pedagogical challenges for the music teacher are actually caused by the varied meanings students attach to music as a social form of expression.

Music teachers may respond to this situation in similar ways as those suggested for music as a compulsory subject, especially as far as the comparative listening projects and the use of electronic keyboards are concerned. Beyond that, the students need hands-on demonstrations by and conversations with real-life musicians, be they composers or performers, both classical and popular. Students also should write and record their own lyrics to familiar tunes and make use of computer software for the development of skills in music theory and basic compositional techniques.

If the teacher chooses the choral experience as the center of performance skill development, the students should study different singing techniques and styles for the purpose of comparison. The teacher might also ask the students to sing songs of their own choice in a stylistically authentic manner. Such performance takes practice. Because it is skill oriented, each student who wishes to showcase his or her own musical preferences and skills should be given time and encouragement to practice those skills, regardless of whether they include rapping or break dancing. All musical skills should be given serious attention by being purposefully practiced.

Throughout such activities, the showing of videos and DVDs of different musical traditions might become routine. However, the excerpts chosen for such purposes should remain short as lengthy viewing and listening leads to the wandering of minds. Student-selected videos and DVDs, always in the context of a particular

---

Small Group Discussion 7.2

What knowledge and skills would you consider to be important in a culturally literate person? Discuss strategies to teach toward such a goal for different school settings.

---

topic and with a very clear time limit set by the teacher, can be another source of listening tasks. The students who present their selections may be asked to talk about their choices in light of the overall instructional objective governing a particular lesson.

Consequences for the Role of Music Teacher

Thinking about formal music schooling in sociological terms lies in understanding why "one size does not fit all," and that, to be effective communicators, music teachers must wear many different hats, each equally important in building and maintaining a successful music program. It is a matter of fully recognizing the sociomusical gestures that define the many different groups with which music teachers come into contact.

Today's music teachers not only are musicians and educators but also public relations managers, arts advocates, and conduits between school and community. To become comfortable with those roles is part and parcel of what makes a school music teacher successful.

In the mid-1960s, Max Kaplan was the first to point out the role complexities in the work music teachers do. He illustrated the relationships between the role of music educator and the educational and political world as depicted in Figure 4.1. He referred to primary and secondary groups not as those that contribute to an educator's own socialization processes during his childhood and adolescence but to the groups with which the adult educator interacts regularly. In doing so, Kaplan used role theory as espoused by functionalists rather than interactionists.

Figure 7.1 is my response to Kaplan's visualization. Beginning with the importance of understanding a music teacher's own socialization process, I use Mead's conceptualization of the "I" and our empirical selves (see Chapter 6), thereby casting a wider net than Kaplan to illustrate how our work plays out in today's schools and local communities. It may become clear that we are not only musician-educators but also sociocultural agents. Musicianship and educatorship together define who we are as music teachers.

The figure is an effort to show the web of interactions that characterizes our daily work. In some instances, we respond to expectations by others; in other cases, we initiate dialogues and communications for making the music program relevant to our students and the school community. To communicate successfully

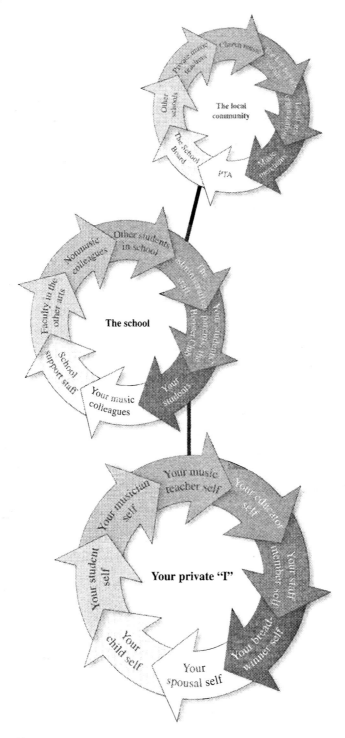

Figure 7.1 Music Teaching from a Micro View: Web of Interactions

The local community

Private music teachers · Church music · Local arts organizations · Local arts council · Music musicians · PTA · The School Board · Other schools

The school

Other students in school · Nonmusic colleagues · Faculty in the other arts · School support staff · Your music colleagues · Your students · Nonstudents: parents, the Booster Club · The administrative, parent staff ·

Your private "I"

Your music teacher self · Your musician self · Your educator self · Your student self · Your staff member self · Your child self · Your bread-winner self · Your spousal self with each of these reference groups and clienteles, we draw in all cases from our own multiple selves, be it by choice or by necessity.

However, the more we know about the values held in the different groups with which we come into contact, be they our students, superiors, or colleagues (music and nonmusic colleagues alike), the easier it is to find strategies by which to reach each of them. It is an acquired skill that depends on our willingness to see ourselves in the midst of ongoing social interactions and socially constructed realities.

8

Conclusion

You and the Big Picture

Honor other personal realities. Find commonalities with yours. Build bridges.

Society is a composite of communities in which different social classes, groups, and reference groups coexist—to varying degrees of compatibility because of real or perceived differences in norms and values as well as hierarchies of power. Informed or intuitive choices made by an individual indicate allegiances to particular groups, how those groups are structured hierarchically, and where and how each individual fits into those hierarchies. The more music teachers are aware of them in their own lives and in the lives of their students, colleagues, and superiors, the more practical sociological knowledge becomes in one's daily teaching.

Sociology is about seeing both the small and the big picture: Who each of us is in the microcosms of our reference groups, imbedded in the macro structure of society. When equally attuned to the bird's-eye view, the bottoms-up approach, and "being in the middle of it," sociological thinking allows us to identify and become familiar with the many layers of interactions that shape each culture, society, family, school, classroom, and rehearsal.

Together, the micro view of the workplace and the macro view of school life in general describe the social complexities inherent in the world of education and music. Seen from those perspectives, the work of music teachers is part of a much larger layering of societal, cultural, educational, and musical purposes. It takes musicianship to feel at home in the sociocultural complexities of music; it takes educatorship to be comfortable with the sociopolitical complexities of formal schooling. Together, musicianship and educatorship determine the actions a teacher chooses during the music instructional process. If one trait appears to dominate over the other, it should only be a matter of where the students are in the process of learning about their musical and personal selves.

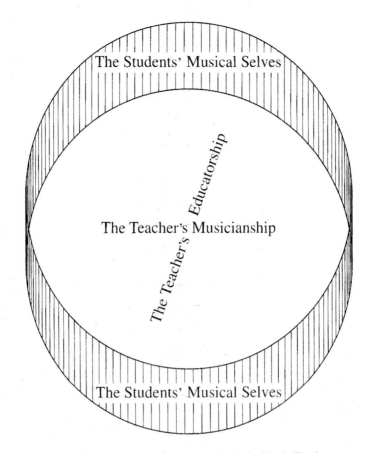

Figure 8.1 Musicianship and Educatorship in the Music Teacher

The dependency between musicianship and educatorship in a good music teacher is depicted in Figure 8.1. It shows how both traits interact with each other as the students get to know their musician selves.

It is often said that music is a universal language. Sociologists might suggest that the word *music* itself is insufficient to communicate its many different meanings, associations, and sounds that people with different musical selves have of the term. Music educators therefore might want to think of music as a universe of languages, made up of different styles and types of sounds shared by different people in different settings.

The settings of greatest significance for school music teachers are those provided by:

- Each teacher's own socialization experiences,
- The students' personal backgrounds and music socialization,
- The students' parents and their sociocultural and musical backgrounds,

- Other music teachers and nonmusic faculty,
- The school administration,
- Professional musicians and amateur musicians connected to the music teacher's own background and music socialization experiences, and
- The school community and the tax-paying political community.

To each of the individuals in the settings, the term *music* triggers certain sound associations that refer to past experiences with music, be it through making or listening to music. The meaning individuals attach to that which they call music signifies who they are, what they value, and with whom they associate or want to be associated.

The social relativity of musical values, acknowledged and pointed out by many sociologists, has caused some writers to fear that sociology means "the ends of arts education" (Dorn, 2003). I believe that such fear is groundless and unsubstantiated because knowledge about the diversity of musical beliefs and value systems within society can actually benefit music teachers by strengthening their roles as music educators and art advocates.

As music educators, we know how to communicate with the students in ways that reflect where each student is socially, musically, and culturally. The musician in us knows how to challenge the students with musical skills and aural models that meet each student's musical capabilities. The musician in us also knows the difference between music as "a mode of self expression" and "as an art form" (Gruhn, 1999), whereas the sociologically savvy pedagogue in us understands how the contextual discrepancy between the two modes can hinder or promote music learning.

As art advocates, our familiarity with the many values and sociocultural meanings that different groups of people attach to their experiences with music leads to improved communication skills. Our power of persuasion thereby becomes strengthened, and we can build arguments that are convincing to nonmusicians.

Finally, to engage our students successfully in the formal acquisition of musical skills and knowledge that become the building blocks for constructing independent musical selves, we should form professional alliances not just within music but also within the world of education. The more collaborative we are in that regard, the more successfully we have applied sociological knowledge to the purpose of music schooling in the context of compulsory education.

What *is* that purpose and how does music fit into it? Agger (2004) answers the first part of the question by asserting that as much as things seem to change from generation to generation, much remains the same: Parents want their children to do well in life and "adolescents are still feeling their way through romantic relationships and friendships. They are still in pursuit of self and community" (p. 5). Schools are expected to provide guidance in all of those pursuits, and music, as so many other subjects, can help in that regard.

In *Brass Performance and Pedagogy* (2002), trumpet performer and pedagogue Keith Johnson calls music a metaphor for all other aspects in life. What one does as a music maker to the best of one's ability, be it as a college-level trumpeter, a second grader listening to and imitating animals in Saint-Saens's *Carnival of the Animals,* a teenager drumming African rhythms in percussion class or humming and moving to a pop tune in general music, a choir singing a medley of Mexican or Brazilian folk songs, or a band fine-tuning excerpts from Copland's *Appalachian Spring,* all of these experiences shape and inform one's life beyond what is learned during the moments that those skills are being honed. As Johnson points out (p. 2), those include both positive and negative experiences, moments of frustration and elation, joyful times and disappointments. They are sensations that, if carefully guided and monitored by the teacher, can give a student a strong sense of self long after high school graduation. That such a sense of self also includes the musician-self is the hope of most music teachers. But the true measure of success lies in the extent to which each individual makes music a lived experience, not a school experience alone.

Definition of Selected Terms

Unless otherwise noted, the definitions are paraphrased or quoted from Abercrombie and Turner (2000).

Community of practice

A real or imaginary place "where skills are acquired, rehearsed, and given value" (English National Board for Nursing, 2000, n.p.)

Conflict theory in education

A theory that analyzes the "tension in society and its parts created by the competing interests of individuals and groups" (Ballantine, 2001, p. 12).

Functionalism

A social theory, originated in the 19th century, that "accounts for a social activity by referring to its consequences for the operation of some other social activity, institution, or society as a whole." Main proponent in the 20th century: Talcott Parsons.

Hidden Curriculum

"The set of values, attitudes or principles that are implicitly conveyed to pupils by teachers. [It] is believed to promote social control at school and in society at large by training people to conform and to obey authority, teaching them to regard social inequalities as natural, [thereby] ensuring cultural reproduction."

Interactionism

The theory derived from Mead's theory of social behaviorism and later called symbolic interaction theory by Blumer (HF). A microsociological theory, similar in many ways to social psychological theories.

See also, *symbolic interaction theory, and social interaction theory*

Musicking

From the invented verb "to musick" to indicate the act of music making and "what it means for the relationships between those who participate in the act at this time, in this place, in this space" *(http://sunsite.queensu.ca/ memorypalace/parlour/Small02/index01.html)*

Occupational identity

The value, meaning, and role behavior one constructs as part of one's work environment (HF).

Role conflict

A term used in various meanings: (1) A person plays two or more roles that are perceived to be incompatible with each other; (2) a person defines a role one way and other persons define it differently; and (3) "related roles have incompatible expectations of the focal role," as can be the case when "supervisors receive conflicting expectations from workers and managers."

Role distance

A term first coined by E. Goffman that "refers to the detachment of the performer from the role he or she is performing."

Social Interaction Theory

First attributed to Erving Goffman (1922–1982), who focused on "the study of social interaction, encounters, gatherings and small groups in *Behavior in Public Places*" (1963). Today the term is often used interchangeably with that of *symbolic interaction theory*. Both theories acknowledge the analytical relationship between the macro and the micro view of society (HF).

Social norm

An expected form of behavior in a given situation. (Dictionary.com, retrieved December 2004 from http://dictionary.reference.com/search? r=2&q=Social%20norm)

Social role

A concept that assumes people's behavior to be "determined mainly by what is expected of the position they hold than by their own individual characteristics."

Socialization

"[T]he process whereby people learn to conform to social norms." It is central to the transmission of a society's culture between generations.

occupational

The process whereby people learn to conform to the norms that define the work for which they get paid (HF).

primary

"The socialization of the young child in the family."

secondary

The socialization that occurs during one's compulsory school years.

Socialization as an adult, "when actors enter roles for which primary and secondary socialization may not have prepared them fully."

Literally, "The study of the processes of companionship. In these terms, sociology may be defined as the study of the bases of social membership."

tertiary/adult

Socialization as an adult "when actors enter roles for which primary and secondary socialization may not have prepared them fully."

Sociology of Education

Originally, the contribution of scholarship in education to issues concerning "social mobility and life-changes, social-class differences in educational attainment and the explanation of these." More recently, issues also include "school ethnographies, . . . descriptions of the social systems of schools, . . . and the significance of pupil-teacher interactions for educational attainment," including "the effectiveness of different teaching styles." Furthermore, "educational sociologists have looked at schools as agencies of cultural reproduction and purveyors of a hidden curriculum" as well as "the role of the school in reinforcing gender stereotypes among children."

Symbolic Interaction Theory

A theoretical tradition that "has its intellectual roots in the concept of the self as developed by George H. Mead, who argued that reflexivity was crucial to the self as a social phenomenon."

References

Abbott, A. (1988). *The system of professions: An essay on the division of export labor*. Chicago: University of Chicago Press.

Abercrombie, N., Hill, S., & Turner, B. (2000). *The Penguin dictionary of sociology* (4th ed.). London: Penguin Books.

Achinstein, B. (2002). *Community, diversity, and conflict among school teachers. The ties that blind*. New York: Teachers College Press.

Adams, M. (Ed.). (1992). *Promoting diversity in college classrooms: Innovative responses for the curriculum, faculty, and institutions*. San Francisco: Jossey-Bass.

Adler, A. (2002). *A case study of boys' experiences of singing in school*. Unpublished doctoral dissertation, University of Toronto.

Adorno, T. (1976). *Introduction to the sociology of music*. Translated from the German by E. B. Ashton. New York: Seabury Press. (Original work published 1962)

Aerni, A., & McGoldrick, K. (Eds.). (1999). *Valuing us all: Feminist pedagogy and economics*. Ann Arbor: University of Michigan Press.

Agger, B. (2004). *The virtual self. A contemporary sociology*. Oxford, England: Blackwell.

Angell, R. (1928). *The campus, a study of contemporary undergraduate life in the American university*. New York: D. Appleton.

Arnold, M. (1924). *Culture and anarchy*. New York: Macmillan. (Original work published 1869)

Asley, B., Cohen, H., & Slatter, R. (1969). *An introduction to the sociology of education*. London: Macmillan.

Ballantine, J. (2001). *The sociology of education. A systematic analysis* (5th ed.). Upper Saddle River, NJ: Prentice Hall.

Baumgarten, A. G. (1961). Aesthetica/scripsit Alexand. Gottlieb Baumgarten. Hildesheim: G. Olms. (Theoretische Ästhetik: die grundlegenden Abschnitte aus der "Aesthetica" (1750/58)/Alexander Gottlieb Baumgarten; übersetzt und herausgegeben von Hans Rudolf Schweizer. Hamburg: Meiner. [Excerpts of *Aesthetica*, translated and edited by H. R. Schweizer])

Becker, H. (1952). The career of the Chicago public school teacher. *American Journal of Sociology, 57* (5), 470–477.

Becker, H. (1963b). The culture of a deviant group: The dance musician. In H. Becker (Ed.), *Outsiders: Studies in the sociology of deviance* (pp. 79–82). New York: Free Press.

Becker, H. (1963a). *Outsiders: Studies in the sociology of deviance.* New York: Free Press.

Becker, H. (1976). Arts worlds and social types. *American Behavioral Scientist, 19* (July), 703–718.

Becker, H. (1977). *Sociological work. Method and substance.* Chicago: Aldine; New Brunswick, NJ: Transaction Books. (Original work published 1970)

Becker, H. (1980). *Role and career problems of the Chicago public school teacher.* New York: Arno Press. (Original work presented as a doctoral dissertation University of Chicago 1951)

Becker, H. (1982). *Art worlds.* Berkeley: University of California Press.

Becker, H., Geer, B., & Hughes, E. (1995). *Making the grade: The academic side of college life.* With a new introduction by H. Becker. New Brunswick, NJ: Transaction Publishers. (Original work published 1968)

Becker, H., Geer, B., Hughes, E., & Strauss, A. (1977). *Boys in white: Student culture in medical school.* Chicago: University of Chicago Press; New Brunswick, NJ: Transaction Books. (Original work published 1961)

Berger, P., & Luckmann, T. (1967). *The social construction of reality. A treatise in the sociology of knowledge.* New York: Doubleday.

Bernstein, B. (1996). *Pedagogy, symbolic control and identity: Theory, research, critique.* London: Taylor & Francis.

Bernstein, B. (2003). *Class, codes and control.* Vols. 1–4: London: Taylor & Francis. (Original work published 1971–1975)

Bidwell, C. (2000). School as context and construction: A social psychological approach to the study of schooling. In M. T. Hallinan (Ed.), *Handbook of the sociology of education* (pp. 15–36). New York: Kluwer Academic/Plenum.

Bidwell, C., Frank, K., & Quiroz, P. (1997). Teacher types, workplace controls, and the organization of schools. *Sociology of Education, 70* (October), 285–307.

Blacking, J. (1967). *Venda children's songs: A study in ethnomusicological analysis.* Johannesburg: Whitwatyersand University Press.

Blacking, J. (1973). *How musical is man?* Seattle: University of Washington Press.

Blumer, H. (1986). *Symbolic interactionism. Perspective and method*. Berkeley: University of California Press. (Original work published 1969)

Blumer, H. (2004). *George Herbert Mead and human conduct*. Edited and introduction by T. J. Morrione. Walnut Creek, CA: AltaMira Press.

Bouije, C. (1998). Swedish music teachers in training and professional life. *International Journal of Music Education, 32*, 24–32.

Bouije, C. (2000). Music teacher socialization: Report from a Swedish Research project. In R. Rideout and S. Paul (Eds.), *On the Sociology of Music Education II*. Papers from the Music Education Symposium at the University of Oklahoma, pp. 51–62. (Privately published Amherst: University of Massachusetts).

Bourdieu, P. (1977). *Outline of a theory of practice*. Translated by Richard Nice. Cambridge: Cambridge University Press.

Bourdieu, P. (1993). *The field of cultural production. Essays on art and literature*. Edited and introduction by Randal Johnson. New York: Columbia University Press.

Bourdieu, P., & Passeron, J. C. (1977). *Reproduction in education, society and culture*. Translated from French by R. Nice. With a foreword by T. Bottomore. London: Sage.

Bourdieu, P., & Wacquant, L. (1992). *An invitation to reflexive sociology*. Chicago: University of Chicago Press.

Bowe, J., Bowe, M., & Streeter, S., with Murphy, D., & Kernochan, R. (Eds.). (2000). *Gig: Americans talk about their jobs at the turn of the millennium*. New York: Crown.

Bowles, S., & Gintis, H. (1976). *Schooling in capitalist America: Educational reform and the contradictions of economic life*. New York: Basic Books.

Bowman, W. (1994). Sound, sociality, and music: Parts One and Two. *The Quarterly Journal of Music Teaching and Learning, 5* (3), 50–59, 60–67.

Bulmer, M. (Ed.). (1977). *Sociological research methods. An introduction*. London: Macmillan Press.

Charon, J. (1998). *Symbolic interactionism: An introduction, an interpretation, an integration* (6th ed.). With a chapter on Erving Goffman by S. Cahill. Upper Saddle River, NJ: Prentice Hall.

Clinton, J. (1997). The self perceptions of certified fine arts teachers toward their roles as artist and instructional staff members in selected public schools of Oklahoma. In R. Rideout (Ed.), *On the sociology of music education* (pp. 121–129). Norman: University of Oklahoma.

Coffman, J. (1971). Everybody knows this is nowhere: Role conflict and the rock musician. *Popular Music in Society, 36* (September), 20–32.

Coleman, J. (1961). *The adolescent society*. With the assistance of J. Johnstone and K. Jonassohn. New York: Free Press of Glencoe.

Coleman, J. (1965). *Adolescents and the schools*. New York: Basic Books.

Collins, R. (1979). *The credential society: Historical sociology of education and stratification*. New York: Academic Press.

Collins, R. (1994). *Four sociological traditions.* Revised and expanded edition of *Three sociological traditions* (1985). New York: Oxford University Press.

Collins, R. (1999). *Macrohistory: Essays in sociology of the long run.* Stanford, CA: Stanford University Press.

Collins, R. (2004). *Interaction ritual chains.* Princeton, NJ: Princeton University Press.

Colwell, R. (Ed.). (1992). *Handbook of research on music teaching and learning.* New York: Schirmer Books.

Colwell, R., & Richardson, C. (Eds.). (2002). *The new handbook of research for music teaching and learning.* New York: Oxford University Press.

Committee on Techniques for the Enhancement of Human Performance: Occupational Analysis, Commission on Behavioral and Social Sciences and Education, National Research Council. (1999). *The changing nature of work. Implications for occupational analysis.* Washington, DC: National Academy Press.

Cooley, C. (1902). *Human nature and the social order.* New York: C. Scribner's Sons.

DaSilva, F., Blasi, A., & Dees, D. (1984). *The sociology of music.* Notre Dame, IN: University of Notre Dame Press.

DeNora, T. (2000). *Music in everyday life.* Cambridge: Cambridge University Press.

DeNora, T. C. (2003). After Adorno: *Rethinking Music Sociology.* Cambridge: Cambridge University Press.

Dewey, J. (1933). *How we think.* Boston: D. C. Heath. (Original work published 1910)

Dorn, C. (2003). Sociology and the end of arts education. *Arts Education Policy Review, 104* (5), 16–24.

Dornbusch, S., & Strober, M. (Eds.). (1988). *Feminism, children, and the new families.* New York: Guilford Press.

Edutopia. Envision the Future of Education. E-Journal: www.edutopia.com

Elliott, D. (1995). *Music matters: A new philosophy of music education.* New York: Oxford University Press.

Elwell, F. (1996). *The sociology of Max Weber.* Retrieved July 28, 2004, from http://www.faculty.rsu.edu/~felwell/Theorists/Weber/Whome.htm

English National Board for Nursing, Midwifery and Health Visiting. (2002). Clinical judgment and nurse education: Nursing identities and communities of practice [abstract]. *Research Highlights,* July.

Engvall, R. (1997). *The professionalization of teaching. Is it truly ado about nothing?* Lanham, NY: University Press of America.

Erikson, K., & Vallas, S. (Eds.). (1990). *The nature of work: Sociological perspectives.* New Haven: Yale University Press.

Etzkorn, K. P. (1966). On esthetic standards and reference groups of popular songwriters. *Sociological Inquiry, 36* (January), 39–47.

Etzkorn, K. P. (Ed.). (1973). *Music and society. The later writings of Paul Honigsheim.* With additional material and bibliographies by K. P. Etzkorn. Foreword by J. A. Beegle. New York: Wiley

Etzkorn, K. P. (Ed.). (1989). *Sociologists and music: An introduction to the study of music and society.* With a new preface and bibliographic update by K. Peter Etzkorn. New Brunswick: Transaction Publishers.

Farnsworth, P. (1969). *The social psychology of music* (2nd ed.). Ames: Iowa State University Press.

Faulkner, R. (1971). *The Hollywood studio musician.* Chicago: Aldine-Atherton Press.

Faulkner, R. (1973). Career concerns and mobility motivations in orchestra musicians. *Sociological Quarterly* (Winter), 334–349.

Feistritzer, C. (1999). *The making of a teacher: A report on teacher preparation in the U.S.* Washington, DC: Center for Education Information.

Feistritzer, C. (2001). C. Emily Feistritzer on teacher preparation. *Edutopia.* Retrieved August 2004 from: www.glef.org/php/interview.php?id= Art_8038&key=039

Feistritzer, C., & Chester, D. (Eds.). (1996). *Profile of teachers in the U.S.* Washington, DC: National Center for Education Information.

Feistritzer, C., & Chester, D. (2001). *Alternative teacher certification: a state-by-state analysis 2001.* Washington, DC: National Center for Education Information.

Fowler, C. (1991). Finding the way to be basic: Music education in the 1990s and beyond. In R. Colwell (Ed.), *Basic Concepts in Music Education, II* (pp. 88–122). Niwot: University Press of Colorado.

Frederickson, J., & Rooney, J. (1988). The free-lance musician as a type of non-person: An extension of the concept of non-personhood. *Sociological Quarterly, 29* (2), 221–239.

Freidson, E. (1986). *Professional powers. A study of the institutionalization of formal knowledge.* Chicago: University of Chicago Press.

Freire, P. (2000). *Pedagogy of the oppressed.* Translated by M. Ramos; with an introduction by D. Macedo. 30th anniversary ed. New York: Continuum. (Original work published 1968; reprinted 1970)

Froehlich, H. (2002). Thoughts on Schools of Music and Colleges of Education as places of "Rites and Rituals": Consequences for research on practicing. In I. M. Hanken, S.G. Nielsen, and M. Nerland (Eds.), *Research in and for higher music education. Festschrift for Harald Jørgensen* (pp. 149–165). Oslo, Norway: Norges musikkhøgskole.

Fussell, P. (1983). *Class.* New York: Ballantine Books.

Gatto, J. (1992). *Dumbing us down: The hidden curriculum of compulsory schooling.* (2005). A special edition with a foreword by Thomos Moore. Philadelphia: New Society Publishers.

Geertz, C. (1973). *The interpretation of cultures: Selected essays.* New York: Basic Books.

Gerth, H., & Mills, C. (Eds.). (1946). *From Max Weber: Essays in sociology.* Translated, edited, and with an introduction by H. H. Gerth and C. Wright Mills. New York: Oxford University Press.

Giroux, H. (1983). *Critical theory & educational practice.* Geelong, Victoria: Deakin University Press/Hyperion Books.

Giroux, H. (1988). *Teachers as intellectuals: Toward a critical pedagogy of learning.* South Hadley, MA: Bergin and Garvey.

Giroux, H. (2004). *The terror of neoliberalism: Authoritarianism and the eclipse of democracy.* Aurora, Canada: Garamond Press.

Goffman, E. (1973). *The presentation of self in everyday life.* Woodstock, NY: Overlook Press. (Original work published 1959)

Green, L. (2001). *How popular musicians learn: A way ahead for music education.* Aldershot, England; Burlington, VT: Ashgate.

Gruhn, W. (1999). Music education in postmodernism. About the difficulties to move knowledge into action, theory into practice. *International Journal of Music Education, 34,* 57–63.

Hamilton, D., & Weiner, G. (2000). Subjects, not subjects: Curriculum pathways, pedagogies and practices in the United Kingdom. Paper presented at the Internationalization of Curriculum Studies Conference, Louisiana State University, Baton Rouge, April 2000. Retrieved December 2004 from http://www.educ.umu.se/~gaby/subjects_not_subjects.html.

Hansen, D., & Gerstl, J. N. (Eds.). (1967). *On education-sociological perspectives.* New York: Wiley.

Hargreaves, D., & North, A. (Eds.). (1997). *Social psychology of music.* Oxford New York: Oxford University Press.

Hebert, D., & Campbell, P. (2000). Rock music in American schools. Positions and practices since the 1960s. *International Journal of Music Education, 36,* 46–57.

Hechter, M., & Horne, C. (2003). *Theories of social order. A reader.* Stanford: Stanford University Press.

Huber, J. (Ed.). (1991). *Macro-micro linkages in sociology.* London: Sage.

Hudak, G., & Kihn, P. (Eds.). (2001). *Labeling: Pedagogy and politics.* London: Routledge/Falmer.

Illich, I. (1971). *Deschooling society.* New York: Harper & Row.

Internet Encyclopedia of Philosophy. (2002). Retrieved August 2003 from http://www.utm.edu/research/iep/.

Johnson, K. (2002). *Brass performance and pedagogy.* Upper Saddle River, NJ: Prentice Hall.

Jorgensen, E. (1997). *In search of music education.* Urbana: University of Illinois Press.

Jorgensen, E. (2003). *Transforming music education.* Bloomington: Indiana University Press.

Kadushin, C. (1969). The professional self-concept of music students. *American Journal of Sociology, 75* (November), 389–404.

Kamerman, J., & Martorella, R. (Eds.). (1983). *Performers & performances: The social organization of artistic work.* New York: Praeger; South Hadley, MA: J. F. Bergin and Garvey.

Kaplan, M. (1990). *The arts. A social perspective.* Rutherford; Madison; Teaneck: Fairleigh Dickinson University Press; London and Toronto: Associated University Press.

Kaplan, M. (1951). *The musician in America: A study of his social roles.* Unpublished thesis. Urbana: University of Illinois.

Kaplan, M. (1952). *A theory of recreational music and current practices in recreational music.* University of Illinois Music Extension Bulletin No. 30. Urbana: Music Extension, Division of University Extension.

Kaplan, M. (1966). *Foundations and frontiers in music education.* New York: Holt, Rinehart & Winston.

Kealy, E. (1974). *The real rock revolution: Sound mixers, social inequality, and the aesthetics of popular music production.* Unpublished doctoral dissertation, Northwestern University.

Kealy, E. (1980). From craft to art: The case of the sound mixers and popular music. *Sociology of Work and Occupations, 6* (September), 3–29.

Keil, C., & Feld, S. (1994). *Music grooves.* Chicago: University of Chicago Press.

Kincheloe, J., & Pinar, W. (1991). *Curriculum as social psychoanalysis: The significance of place.* Albany: State University of New York Press.

L'Roy, D. (1983). *The development of occupational identity in undergraduate music education majors.* Unpublished doctoral dissertation, Denton: North Texas State University [University of North Texas].

Lamb, R., Dolloff, L., & Howe, S. (2002). Feminism, feminist research, and gender research in music education: A selective review. In R. Colwell and C. Richardson (Eds.), *The new handbook of research for music teaching and learning* (pp. 648–674). New York: Oxford University Press.

Legassé, P. (Ed.). (2001). *The Columbia encyclopedia* (6th ed.). New York: Columbia University Press; [Detroit, Mich.]: Sold and distributed by Gale Group, ©2000.

Leppert, R., & McClary, S. (1987). *Music and society: The politics of composition, performance and reception.* Cambridge [Cambridgeshire]: Cambridge University Press.

Lipset, M., & Hofstadter, R. (1968). *Sociology and history: Methods.* New York: Basic Books.

Lortie, D. (1959). Laymen to lawmen: Law school, careers, and socialization. *Harvard Educational Review, 29,* 155–171.

Lortie, D. (2002). *The schoolteacher: A sociological study.* With new introduction. Chicago: University of Chicago Press. (Original work published 1975)

Lundquist, B. (1984a). Socialization and music: Some directions for research. Presentation at the Social Behavior/Anthropology Special Research Interest Group, MENC In-service conference, Chicago, March 21–24, 1984.

Lundquist, B. (1984b). *A sociomusical research agenda for music in higher education.* Paper presented at the National Association of Schools of Music annual conference, Washington, DC, November 19, 1984.

MacDonald, R., Hargreaves, D., & Miell, D. (Eds.). (2002). *Musical identities.* Oxford: Oxford University Press.

Mark, D. (1998). The music teacher's dilemma—musician or teacher. *International Journal of Music Education, 32,* 3–23.

Martin, P. (1995). *Sounds and society. Themes in the sociology of music.* Manchester: Manchester University Press.

Mazur, R. (2002). *Dictionary of critical sociology.* Retrieved August 2, 2002, from http://www.public.iastate.edu/~rmazur/dictionary/a.html.

McCall, G., & Simmons, J. (1978). *Identities and interactions: An examination of human associations in everyday life.* New York: The Free Press.

McCarthy, M. (1997). The foundations of sociology in American music education (1900–1935). In R. Rideout (Ed.), *On the sociology of music education* (pp. 71–80). Norman: University of Oklahoma.

McClary, S. (1991). *Feminine endings: Music, gender and sexuality.* Minneapolis: University of Minnesota Press.

McClary, S. (2000). *Conventional wisdom. The content of musical form.* Berkeley: University of California Press.

Mead, G. H. (1938). *The philosophy of the act.* Edited, with introduction, by C. Morris, in collaboration with J. Brewster, A. Dunham, & D. Miller. Chicago: University of Chicago Press.

Merton, R. (1957). *Social theory and social structure. Toward the codification of theory and research* (revised and enlarged ed.). Glencoe, IL: Free Press.

Merton, R. (1967). *Social theory and social structure. Part I. On theoretical sociology; five essays, old and new.* New York: Free Press.

Meighan, R., & Siraj-Blatchford, I. (2003). *A sociology of educating* (4th ed.). With contributions by L. Barton and S. Walker. London: Continuum.

Middleton, R. (1990). *Studying popular music.* Buckingham: Open University Press.

Mueller, J. (1958). Music and education: A sociological approach. In N. B. Henry (Ed.), *Basic concepts in music education* (pp. 88–122). Chicago: National Society for the Study of Education; distributed by the University of Chicago Press, 1958.

Nash, D. (1954). *The American composer. A study in social psychology.* Unpublished thesis, University of Pennsylvania.

Nash, D. (1957). The socialization of an artist: The American composer. *Social Forces, 35* (Spring), 307–313.

Nash, D. (1961). The role of the composer. *Ethnomusicology, 5* (September), 81–94; 187–205.

Nielsen, K. (1999). *Musical apprenticeship. Learning at the Academy of Music as socially situated.* Doctoral dissertation. Aarhus: Aarhus University, Institute of Psychology.

North, A., Hargreaves, D., & Tarrant, M. (2002). Social psychology and music education. In R. Colwell and C. Richardson (Eds.), *The new handbook for research on music teaching and learning* (pp. 604–625). New York: Oxford University Press.

O'Toole, P. (1997a). Escaping the traditions: Tensions between the production of values and pleasures in the choral setting. In R. Rideout (Ed.), *On the sociology of music education* (pp. 130–148). Norman: University of Oklahoma.

O'Toole, P. (1997b). Examining the political projects of four pedagogies: Progressive humanistic, critical, and feminist. *Dialogue in Instrumental Music Education, 21* (2), 126–141.

O'Toole, P. (1998). A missing chapter from choral methods books: How choirs neglect girls. *Choral Journal, 39* (5), 9–32.

Olmedo, I. (1997). Challenging old assumptions: Preparing teachers for inner city school. *Teaching and Teacher Education, 13* (3), 245–258.

Parsons, T. (1937). *The structure of social action; a study in social theory with special reference to a group of recent European writers.* New York: McGraw-Hill.

Parsons, T. (1951). *The social system.* Glencoe, IL: Free Press.

Pavalko, R. (1971). *Sociology of occupations and professions.* Itasca, IL: F. E. Peacock.

Pavalko, R. (1972a). Recruitment to teaching: Patterns of selection and retention. In R. M. Pavalko (Ed.), *Sociological perspectives on occupations* (pp. 239–249). Itasca, IL: F. E. Peacock.

Pavalko, R. (Ed.). (1972b). *Sociological perspectives on occupations.* Itasca, IL: F. E. Peacock.

Randel, D. (Ed.). (1999). *Harvard concise dictionary of music and musicians.* Cambridge, MA: Belknap Press.

Regelski, T. (1998). Critical theory as a basis for critical thinking in music education. In P. Woodford (Ed.). *Studies in music from the University of Western Ontario* (Vol. 17). (pp 1–21). London, Ontario: University of Western Ontario.

Regelski, T. (2004). *Teaching general music in grades 4–8. A musicianship approach.* New York: Oxford University Press.

Riedel, J. (1964). The function of sociability in the sociology of music and music education. *Journal of Research in Music Education, 12* (2), 149–158.

Roberts, B. (1991a). *A place to play. The social world of university schools of music.* St. John's: Memorial University of Newfoundland, Faculty of Education.

Roberts, B. (1991b). *Musician. A process of labelling.* St. John's: Memorial University of Newfoundland, Faculty of Education.

Roberts, B. (1993). *I, musician. Towards a model of identity construction and maintenance by music education students as musicians.* St. John's: Memorial University of Newfoundland Faculty of Education.

Roberts, B. (1994). Music teachers as researchers. *International Journal of Music Education, 23,* 24–33.

Roberts, B. (2000). Gatekeepers and the reproduction of institutional realities: The case of music education in Canadian universities. In H. Froehlich and K. Chesky (Eds.), *The education of the professional musician,* A special issue of *Musical Performance, 2* (3), 63–80.

Roberts, B. (2004). Who's in the mirror? Issues surrounding the identity construction of music educators. Retrieved August 2004 from http:// www.siue. edu/MUSIC/ACTPAPERS/v3/roberts04b.htm.

Scruton, R. (1980). *The meaning of conservatism.* Totowa, NJ: Barnes & Noble Books.

Scruton, R. (2000). *An intelligent person's guide to modern culture.* South Bend, IN: St. Augustine's Press.

Seeger, C. (1977). *Studies in musicology, 1935–1975.* Berkeley: University of California Press.

Seeger, C. (1994). *Studies in musicology II, 1929–1979.* Edited and with an introduction by Ann M. Pescatello. Berkeley: University of California Press.

Shepherd, J. (1991). *Music as social text.* Cambridge: Polity Press.

Shepherd, J., & Wicke, P. (1997). *Music and cultural theory.* Cambridge, UK: Polity Press; Malden, MA: Published in the United States by Blackwell.

Shepherd, J., Berden P., Vulliamy, G., Wishart, T. (1977). *Whose music? A sociology of musical languages.* London: Latimer.

Shibutani, T. (1987). *Society and personality; an interactionist approach to social psychology.* With a new preface by Barry Glassner. New Brunswick, NJ: Transaction Books.

Siegmeister, E. (1974). *Music and society.* New York: Haskell House. (Original work published 1938)

Silbermann, A. (1963). *Sociology of music.* Translated by C. Stewart. London: Routledge & Kegan Paul. (Original work published 1957)

Simpson, I. (1972). Patterns of socialization into professions: The case of student nurses. In R. Pavalko (Ed.), *Sociological perspectives on occupations* (pp. 169–177). Reprinted from *Sociological Inquiry, 37* (Winter 1967), 47–59.

Small, C. (1977). *Music-society-education. A radical examination of the prophetic function of music in Western, Eastern and African cultures with its impact on society and its use in education.* New York: Schirmer. (Reprinted in 1996 as *Music, society, education.* With a new foreword by Robert Walser. London: Calder.

Small, C. (1998a). *Musicking. The meanings of performing and listening.* Hanover, NH: University Press of New England.

Small, C. (1998b). *Music of the common tongue. Survival and celebration in African American music.* Hanover, NH: University Press of New England. (Original work published 1987)

Southern, E. (1997). *The music of black Americans: A history* (3rd ed.). New York: Norton. (Original work published 1971)

Stebbins, R. (1964). *The jazz community: The sociology of a musical sub-culture.* Unpublished doctoral dissertation, University of Minnesota.

Stebbins, R. (1966). Class, status, and power among jazz and commercial musicians. *Sociological Quarterly, 7* (Winter), 197–213.

Stephens, J. (1993). Artist or teacher? *International Journal of Music Education, 25,* 3–13.

Stewart, C. (1992). Who takes music? Investigating access to high school music as a function of social and school factors (social factors). Unpublished doctoral dissertation, University of Michigan, 1991. *Dissertation Abstracts International 52/10,* p. 3554.

Straus, M., & Nelson, J. (1968). *Sociological analysis. An empirical approach through replication.* New York: Harper & Row.

Supičić, I. (1987). *Music in society: A guide to the sociology of music.* New York: Pendragon Press. (Original work published 1964; reprinted in 1971)

Taylor, S., & Sobel, D. (2001). Addressing the discontinuity of students' and teachers' diversity: A preliminary study of preservice teachers' beliefs and perceived skills. *Teaching and Teacher Education, 17* (4), 478–503.

Tepperman, L., & Rosenberg, M. (1998). *Macro/micro: A brief introduction to sociology* (3rd ed.). Toronto: Prentice-Hall.

Vulliamy, G., & Lee, E. (Eds.). (1976). *Pop music in school.* Cambridge and New York: Cambridge University Press.

Weber, M. (1958). *The rational and social foundations of music.* Translated and edited by D. Martindale, J. Riedel, and G. Neuwirth. Carbondale: Southern Illinois University Press. (Original work published 1921)

Weber, M. (2002). *The Protestant ethic and the "spirit" of capitalism and other writings by Max Weber.* Edited, translated, and with an introduction by P. Baehr and G. Wells. New York and London: Penguin Books. (Original work published 1905; revised 1920)

White, H. (1964). *The professional role and status of the school music teacher in American society.* Unpublished doctoral dissertation, University of Kansas, Lawrence.

White, H. (1967). The professional role and status of the school music teacher in American Society. *Journal of Research in Music Education 15* (1) 3–10.

Wiggins, R., & Follow, E. (1999). Development of knowledge, attitudes, and commitment to teach diverse student populations. *Journal of Teacher Education, 50* (2), 94–105.

Woodford, P. (2005). Democracy and music education: Liberalism, ethics, and the politics of practice. Bloomington: Indiana University Press.

Web Sites

The web sites listed here are those referenced as footnotes in the text and intended for further browsing and exploration. Where not indicated otherwise, most of them were retrieved as listed between June to August 2004. Not all of the sites are available anymore; however, where they have new addresses, the most recent web site addresses are listed as well.

http://home.earthlinnk.net/~hsbecker/ *See now:*
http://socsci.colorado.edu/SOC/SI/si-becker.htm

http://www.public.iastate.edu~mazur/dictionary/html *See now:*
library.csu.edu/guides/subjects/**sociology**.pdf

http://www.brock.uni-wuppertal.de/Schrifte/English/Mediatio.html

http://www.educ.umu.se/~gaby/subjects_not_subjects.html

http://glef.org/php/interview.php?id=Art_803&key=039 *See now:*
http://www.edutopia.org/php/interview.php?id=Art_803

http://www.humnet.ucla.edu/humnet/musicology/faculty-bios/mcclary.html

http://www.nyu.edu/educaton/music/mayday/maydaygroup/index.htm *See now:*
http://www.maydaygroup.org/

http://www.osviews.com/modules.php?op=modload&name=News&file=article&sid=719

http://sapir.ukc.ac.uk/QUB/Introduction/I_Frame.html

http://www.siue.edu/MUSIC/ACTPAPERS/v3/Roberts04b.htm *See now*:
http://www.maydaygroup.org/ACT/v3n2/Roberts04b.pdf

http://www.src.uchicago.edu/ssr1/PRELIMS/Theory/parsons.html

http://www.stanford.edu/~myras/pdf_docs/fem_econ.pdf, retrieved December 2004.

Index of Selected Names
and Terms

Follow, E., 17
Foundations and Frontiers of Music Education (Kaplan), 4, 57–58
Fowler, C., 6
Frank, K., 32
Frankfurt school of critical theory, 53, 59
Frederickson, J., 9
Freidson, E., 21
Freire, P., 82, 83
Froehlich, H., 15
Functionalist theory/theorists in education, 80–82
  social issues/school instruction and, 92–98
"Function of Sociability in the Sociology of Music and Music Education, The" (Riedel), 52
Fussel, P., 12

G

Gatto, J., 85
Geer, B., 27
Geertz, C., 65
Gerstl, J., 79
Gerth, H., 53
Gintis, H., 12
Giroux, H, 86, 95
Goffman, E., 24, 90
Green, L., 100
Gruhn, W., 24, 117

H

Hamilton, D., 85
Hansen, D., 79
Hargreaves, D., 6, 7
Harvard Concise Dictionary of Music and Musicians (Randel), 66
Hebert, D., 4
Hechter, D., 44
Hegel, G.W.F., 54
Hidden curriculum, 84–85
  power behind, 96–98
  in school music, 104–9
Hierarchies of power, 21–22, 25
Hierarchy of positions, 22
High culture, Scruton on, 72–74
Hill, S., 86

Hofstadter, R., 44
Honigsheim, P., 59–60
Horkheimer, M., 53
Horne, C., 44
Howe, S., 109
How Musical Is Man? (Blacking), 68
Huber, J., 44
Hudak, G., 91
Hughes, E., 27
Human Nature and the Social Older (Cooley), 87

I

Illich, I., 82, 83
Institutional objectives, 21
Instructional objectives, 21
Interactionism, 87
Interactionist theory/theorists, 45–47
  contemporary, 90
  in education, 80, 87–89
  in music education, 48, 49
  social issues/school instruction and, 92–98
Internet Encyclopedia of Philosophy, The, 88
Introduction to a Sociology of Music (Adorno), 55

J

James, W., 87
Johnson, K., 117
Jorgensen, E., 76
Journal of Research for Music Education, 52

K

Kadushin, C., 12–13
Kamerman, J., 9
Kaplan, M., 4, 112
  music education and, 62
  on sociology of music, 57–59
Kealy, E., 9
Keil, C., 75
Kernochan, R., 21
Kihn, P., 91
Kincheloe, J., 109
Kodály, Z., 15, 23, 75, 100

occupational socialization, 12–14
  social roles, 24–25
Music Teachers National Association, 8

N

Nash, D., 9
National Association for Music Educa-
    tion (MENC), 109
National Educational Association
    (NEA), 8
National Jazz Educators Association, 8
Nature of institutional work (Becker),
    27–28
Nelson, J., 44
Nielsen, K., 15
Non-participant observational
    methods, 47
Normative culture, 24
Norms, 16. *See* Social norms
North, A., 6

O

Occupation, defined, 21
Occupational identity
    defined, 7
    musicians and, 7–18
Occupational norms and values, 23–24
Occupational socialization, 7, 21–23
    of music students, 12–15
    overview, 21–23
    subject matter and, 34–36
Olmedo, I., 17
Orff, C., 15, 23, 75, 100
Organization of American Kodály Edu-
    cators, 8, 75
O'Toole, P., 109

P

Parsons, T., 24, 81
Participant observation, 47
Passeron, J.C., 85, 93
Pavalko, R., 11, 21, 34, 35
    on teacher self-selection/retention,
        12, 28–29
Peirce, C.S., 87
Philosophy of the Act, The (Mead), 88

Pinar, W., 109
Primary groups, 88
Primary socialization, 7
Professional, concept of, 21–22
Professionalism, 23
Professional performers. *See* Musicians
"Professional Role and Status of the
    School Music Teacher in
    American Society"
    (White), 15
*Protestant Ethic and the Spirit of
    Capitalism, The* (Weber), 52

Q

Quiroz, P., 32

R

Randel, D., 66
*Rational and Social Foundations of Mu-
    sic, The* (Weber), 52
Rationalization, Weber's theory of,
    52–53
Reference group theory, 91
Reflexive sociology, 85
Regelski,T., 75, 102
Richardson, C., 5
Riedel, J., 52
Roberts, B., 13–14, 49
Role conflict, 25
Role distance, 25
Role expectations, 25
Role playing, 89
Role taking, 89
Role theory, 24
Rooney, J., 9
Rosenberg, M., 45

S

"School as Context and Construction:
    A Social Psychological
    Approach to the Study of
    Schooling" (Bidwell), 32, 33
Schooling, education distinguished from,
    95–96. *See also* Music
    schooling
Schoolteacher: A Sociological Study
    (Lortie), 29